The Blues and I

An Autobiography

Kevin Ratcliffe

To Tommy
Best Wishes

ARTHUR BARKER
Weidenfeld and Nicolson
London

Published in Great Britain by
George Weidenfeld & Nicolson Ltd
91 Clapham High Street
London SW4 7TA

ISBN 0 213 16959 2

Photoset by Deltatype Ellesmere Port

Printed in Great Britain by
Butler & Tanner Ltd, Frome and London

Contents

Illustrations

Illustrations

The photographs in this book come from the author's collection unless otherwise stated.

To Dad for giving me a dream. To Sharon, Mum and family for having the patience to let me see it through. To Colin Harvey and the rest of the Everton lads for helping me make it come true.

1

Cinderella Time

If anyone had told me back in 1982 that I would be writing my life story now, I would have told them they were nuts. I would also have bet them that if I did write it, none of the six years would involve Everton. At that time, I was so unhappy at Goodison that I couldn't wait to get away. My relationship with manager Howard Kendall was bad. I was close to hating him. And my career was heading nowhere. If a decent club had come for me, I'd have gone; and this story would have been very different. The trouble was simple but, for me, soul destroying. The club were deep in trouble and yet they weren't using me. I was twenty-two, a full Welsh international, yet they couldn't see that under their noses was someone with a bit of talent who was desperate to help them out, and prove himself. No one was ever more frustrated, and I couldn't see that situation changing.

Now, when I look back, the transformation for the club and me is so unbelievably startling that it looks more like something out of a fairy tale like *Cinderella* than soccer. The club have climbed out of the mire and into the most successful period of their history – with me as captain! And, after being so far out in the cold there could have been icicles on my boots,

I'm in my testimonial year which signifies ten years' service for the club. What has been achieved in such a short time is almost miraculous.

Everton have known more than a few purple periods in their 110 years, but the club had been living under two huge shadows, the red one of Liverpool and the blue one of Harry Catterick's legendary 1970 Everton champions. Those shadows, if any remain, have been reduced to pocket size. For too long our supporters had only memories of the Ball-Harvey-Kendall team to keep them going during the bad times. They had to take years of insults from the reds across Stanley Park while we struggled, and it must have been hard for them to stay loyal. But we have given them the chance to stick their chests out with pride again over the last few years, winning championships, the European Cup Winners' Cup, the FA Cup, the Charity Shield and, along the way, making Wembley seem like a home ground. As for me, add to all that the honour of being captain of a club that has been part of my life since I needed a soapbox to stand on when I first watched them, and you may begin to see why I bring *Cinderella* into it. Howard Kendall said when we were heading for Wembley in 1984, 'This is the year of the Rats.' As far as I'm concerned, every year since has been the same. There's more to come before I'm finished, but if it all had to end now, I couldn't complain. Winning championships and medals and playing for your country aren't natural expectations of a lad from Mancot, my little village in North Wales.

I was born there on the 12th November 1960, eleven months ahead of my brother, Paul, and eight years before my sister, Helen. I still live only a mile away and that kind of loyalty to the area is typical of the local people. Everybody knows everybody else. I had a great childhood, happy and secure. We weren't rich. My dad, Brian, was a joiner and my mum, Hannah, a school cleaner, but whatever we wanted we usually got. Dad kept a belt but needed no more than to bring it out if there was any messing about. It was there only as a frightener. Paul and I would fight like hell, and we used to have real boxing sessions, with proper gloves, on Sunday mornings in the front room. Dad was the timekeeper using a little brass gong, and after we'd finished with each other we'd end up going for him! Mum preferred to look after the budgie than bother with this daft men's business.

Dad never mentioned sticking an Everton rosette on my pram but I wouldn't be surprised if he did. He was – and is – a fanatic, who drives my wife, Sharon, mad with his endless football talk. And I suppose I should be relieved I wasn't christened with names like Kendall, Harvey, Ball, Labone, Royle, Husband, Hurst, etc. I remember a Liverpool fan inflicted on his poor child the names of one of Bill Shankly's teams. Certainly, supporting the right team was part of Dad's way of upbringing and he made sure I looked at quality from the start. When I was about eight years old he took me to Goodison Park with three of his brothers and a neighbour. And it was there that I was riveted by Alan Ball. The little redhead could do no wrong for me. He was so cheeky that he even sat on the ball during one game when Everton were so on top that they were just strolling about. Another picture that's stuck in my mind is of little Johnny Morrissey taking people on down the wing and big Joe Royle sticking in the centres. There haven't been many better introductions to the game than mine. Dad only took me to Everton and certainly wouldn't let me watch Liverpool. I can't even remember Liverpool being mentioned in our household. For me, it was always Everton or Wrexham. I used to go to the Racecourse ground a lot and once ran on the pitch and was really chuffed to grab David Smallman's old tie-up.

There's no doubt I got my ability from Dad although maybe not my competitive attitude. I'm told that if someone kicked my dad up in the air then that was the end of them! Dad would love to have made a career at Goodison. He was a left-winger who, he tells me, could put his crosses on a sixpence. But the nearest he got to his dream was playing for Everton C and D teams and Manchester City reserves, so I hope he's been able to live through me a little of what he could never have himself. Despite his own frustrations, he never pushed us towards football. He would encourage Paul and me and get the ball out whenever we wanted, but there was no pressure. If anything, Paul was more dedicated to football than I was, but maybe the game came more naturally to me. Life can be cruel that way. But Paul's played non-league football and he doesn't begrudge whatever I've got from the game. Far from it. He's been a terrific supporter.

It was lucky for me that football did come naturally because I don't know what else I would have done. I wasn't good at classroom work, finishing with a few moderate CSEs. And there's no way I could have gone to work with Dad at his joinery. I was hopeless at metalwork and woodwork, and even if I had been good with my hands, I would have been put off by what happened when Paul tried it. Almost every night the pair of them would come home arguing about some silly thing or another. And I couldn't have sat in an office all day for all the money in the world. No, if it hadn't been football, it would have had to be labouring, lorry driving, or painting and decorating. And if I'd had to change my sport it would have meant switching to rugby. I loved the game at school, but Everton's youth development officer, Ray Minshull, warned me off even before I signed on as an apprentice.

How about running, I hear you say. Well, I may be known as one of the fastest defenders in the business, but at school I hated running as a sport. I loved watching it, but just could not stand doing it. I set school records for the short sprints. At thirteen, I was doing just over 13 seconds for the 100 and at fourteen, I was doing the 200 in 24.5 seconds. But I didn't enjoy it. In fact, I had to be forced into it. Teachers got me going with one very good bribe which went, 'If you don't do athletics, you don't play football.' But they could never get me to run for the county. I understood their motives. They wanted the best for the school but athletics just didn't interest me. Speed is one of those things given to you. Kevin Sheedy would probably say the same about his passing. You've either got it, or you haven't. But testing speed for testing's sake doesn't interest me. When people like Ian Snodin and Pat Van den Hauwe come to the club, they hear about me and start putting out challenges. But I say, 'If you want a race, try Gary Stevens.' Now there's a man who could have been a tremendous athlete. I'm just not bothered about showing my pace anywhere but where it counts – on the pitch. As long as that speed is there when I need it, that's all that matters. I must say when I see things like the Olympics and Ben Johnson screaming away in the sprints, I catch myself wondering what might have happened if I'd worked at it. But that's as far as it goes.

Everton are not a club where everybody's trying to beat everybody else. That's where the team strength comes in. Apart from as a 'wind-up', nobody's bothered who's the quickest, the best passer, or the best goal scorer, as long as the team's doing well. That's where the fighting for each other comes in. If I had to go to war, I'd rather be in a group with Everton players than any others. I know that I could always look behind me and know the rest would be there as back-up. And that's a good feeling. Everybody wants to be successful and everybody wants to work for each other. Newcomers just can't believe what a great bunch they have come to. Ian Snodin thought he'd been with a good set of lads at Leeds, but it opened his eyes how well we got on. I'm not exaggeerating when I say that it is a joy to go into training. Players elsewhere will wake up and not like the idea of going into work at all, and I pity them. That's a feeling I've not known at Everton even in my blackest days.

2

Down to Basics

I learned my soccer basics on the worst pitch in the world. There were supposed to be old mineshafts there and I suppose there was a risk any of us might suddenly disappear. But the thought never crossed our minds. It was rough but it was heaven to us. Every day, all the boys in the street used to go up to what we knew as the 'top fields'. I would have been eight or nine years old, playing mainly against boys of thirteen or fourteen. Sombody would get a ball and if it bust, we'd all chip in for another. That's something you don't see now. We used to have a great laugh but we made it as near the real thing as we could, even digging out a trainer's dug-out and putting a corrugated iron sheet over it. One day, we were devastated to go up there, ready for our usual game, to find six-feet deep holes had been dug all over our pitch. Surveyors had come to test the area to see how safe it was for housing, which is what is on there now. Not surprisingly, they met a little local resistance. When they came back the next day, they found all their holes filled in, apart from our dug-out, of course. It was our pitch and we didn't want it taken from us.

From the start, I used to set myself career targets. Every time I achieved one target I'd be looking to the next, and that's the way it was until I played for Everton's first team. That last one was to be achieved by the time I was nineteen. If not, I'd be away to try my luck elsewhere. I think I got in when I was nineteen and a half!

My first ambition was to play for Deeside Primaries. That was the main under-eleven team in the area and run by a great fella, Ron Bishop. Another early aim was to get in the Sunday team run by my uncles, Colin and Neville. They were semi-cripples, but nobody could have put more into their Deeside Athletic. The family used to muck in and help. Dad put up the nets with my grandad and another uncle, Graham. Sometimes Dad and Graham played alongside me. Just the name 'Deeside' made it sound special, and everyone wanted to join. There were some good players there. The spirit was terrific and my uncles made sure that it stayed that way. Everyone was given a medal at the end of the year even if they hadn't won anything. But usually we did win. In four years, they went from division D to A of the Chester League. I still used to turn out for them after I'd signed schoolboy forms with Everton. I would play in Everton's A or B teams on the Saturday and then for my uncles on Sunday. People used to say to me 'you don't need Sunday football now.' But I loved it. I can remember some of those games more vividly now than I can many Everton games.

It was an important part of my football education, too. I was a midfielder then and coming up against tough twenty-year-old steelworkers and miners was an experience. I wasn't the smallest fifteen-year-old but they could be big, very big. I remember getting sent off in a cup match after a punch up. This lad came on as sub and started kicking lumps out of our guys. Well, I was going through, went into a tackle, and he kicked me. I turned round and a fight broke out. He was in his twenties but that didn't come into it. I had a go and both of us ended up taking the long walk. I think Dad was more upset than me, but it was just one of those things. Punishment in games is something you have to accept and I found that hard.

But you have to learn that if you give it out, a certain amount is going to come back. Playing in that team did help. It brought me on a step. Even today I still get reminded about that incident if I go out for a drink with Geoff Pearson and Gareth Thomas, lads who played alongside me in those days.

Schoolboy honours came fast – Flint and District, Clwyd, Wales – and, after one game in the national under-fifteen side, I was being described in the Wembley programme for the England match as 'a powerful defender who reads the game like a veteran.' It made nice reading but maybe 60,000 screaming kids there wondered what all that was about. England won 4–1 and a certain Wayne Clarke, who seemed to have half the clubs in the land chasing him, laid on two. England were so strong they could play Andy Ritchie and leave Clive Allen on the bench for half the game. Quite a few others of that England side have made good careers in the pro game – Mike Fillery, Phil Brignull, Brendan Ormsby. Who made it from ours? Just two – Tarki Micallef and me. Mark Botto, Mark Hanson and Paul Lewis all signed for Everton but were released. I must say I was surprised when Mark Hanson wasn't kept on. He was the bravest keeper I've seen. I remember him diving at the feet of a lad against Liverpool after he'd dislocated his jaw. When he was released that was the last I saw of him until the League Cup final with Liverpool. We were just on our way to the Wembley dressing-room when up stepped this policeman and called to us. It was Mark. He was on duty there! Everybody had been over the moon about another of my under-fifteen team-mates, midfielder David Haggett. He was good and Manchester United signed him, but he never made it. He was in their B team when I was in Everton's reserves.

Success in this game comes from more than ability. Work, perseverance and luck are just as important. I wouldn't say I was a natural player, although some things did come naturally. Anybody who'd seen me play at left-back for

Everton in my early days probably said, 'He'll never make a player.' But I was determined to get there. It only looks as if you've got a gift if you've played a few years, been successful and drawn confidence from that. The luck comes at being in the right place when opportunity knocks, although I'm also a believer in making your own luck. Perseverance? I had five centre-halves ahead of me at Everton – David Jones, Roger Kenyon, Mick Lyons, Mark Higgins, Billy Wright. And that was the test I nearly failed.

Although I was such a fan, it wasn't a certainty that I'd go to Everton as a kid. Manchester City, Spurs, Burnley and Wrexham were all interested. And I could very easily have been with Ian Rush at Chester. Liverpool? Dad wouldn't have let them near the door, let alone through it! In those early days, everyone from our area seemed to be getting shipped off to Burnley for trials. They had a scout, Harold Wainwright, and he would say to me. 'You'll have to come to Burnley.' But that's all I did hear from him for two years – in fact, not until the day I was going down to Spurs on trial. The phone rang. It was Harold. 'You coming down to Burnley?' he asked. 'Sorry,' I said, 'it's taken you all this time to get round to it. I'm off to Tottenham.'

So I went to White Hart Lane for a week – and I did not like it at all. Tarki Micallef was there at the same time. They looked after us well and coach, Ron Henry, left-back in the great double side of the 1960s, was good to me although he gave the apprentices some terrible stick. But I could not get rid of the feeling that it was not a part of the country that I could ever feel at home in. Mark Kendall, an apprentice there, used to show us around and did his best, but that area of North London is rough and I did not fancy it. My general impression of the club also wasn't helped by Martin Chivers. I was taken to a reserves match on the team bus. Chivers, Glenn Hoddle (who would have been very young then) and Neil McNab were all playing. It was about a year after Chivers had played the last of his twenty-four games for England and he was still a big target for the autograph hunters. But he wouldn't have it, pushing them away as if there was a smell under his nose. Even at fifteen, I was annoyed by the arrogance of the man. When I came home, I said to my father, 'They want me to go back for another trial but I don't fancy it.' As it was left to me, that was the end of my Spurs career.

In a way, it was such a shame because Spurs could not have done more for me as a club. There was no quibbling about expenses. They even paid for my parents and me to go down to watch a game. They also caused one of my more embarrassing experiences, and with the best of intentions. They knew I was an Everton fan and when Spurs came up to Goodison to play they offered me tickets. I didn't need asking twice. On the day of the match, I arrived with my brother, Paul, and my big mate, Steven 'Jakey' Jacques. Sure enough, the tickets had been left for me by Spurs manager Terry Neill. Great – until I saw where they were for. Only the directors' box! And we were dressed for the terraces, weren't we! I was in my Doc Marten boots and flared pants. The others were in scruffy jeans. And, of course, we all had our Everton scarves. All this was decorating the front row of the bigwigs' box! We tried to keep a low profile, but that wasn't easy in our get-up and considering where we were. They must have wondered who those scruffy beggars were. Anyway, we dared not go down to the lounge for a half-time cup of tea!

Manchester City was the next stop on my tour of possibles. And, again, a week was more than enough to say 'no thanks.' I was lucky that a couple of other Welsh lads were there because I felt I had intruded into a clique who didn't want any outsiders. It was a matter of 'us and them' and I was glad that one of the Welsh lads was big, tough and showed he was willing to stand up and be counted if necessary. To cap it all, I didn't get any expenses.

Wrexham was also a possibility for me, and I went for a few

trials there. I was a bit of a fan and they were good to me, but I didn't fancy it. It was just a feeling on my part that turned me against them. So, in the end, it was between Chester and Everton. I was training with both. And, believe it or not, that was a tough choice, particularly because Chester had Cliff Sear in charge of the kids. He was the one who had a lot to do with bringing on Rushy, who was to be signed a year later, and he is a genuinely nice fella. He said he'd give his right arm for me and probably meant it. Both clubs pushed hard for an answer, especially Everton. The pressure was probably exerted more on Dad than me, not only in the obvious sense but through feelings complicated by his love of Everton and wish to do what was best for me. He did not influence me. In fact, he seemed to lean Chester's way on the grounds of quicker opportunity.

This all went on over two years of school holidays and, looking back, I thought I kept my feet on the ground pretty well while all these clubs were chasing me. The thing was that I had to get it right in my own mind, and the way it's turned out, despite a big hiccup in the middle, the final decision was right. I made my mind up straight after playing at Chester one night. On the way home, the usual conversation started in the car. 'They want you to sign,' said Dad. But this time I cut it short, saying, 'I'll sign for Everton.' There was a short, stunned silence and then, 'Are you sure you want to do that? Don't you think you'd be better off at Chester?' These were very fair questions from an Everton fan but I'd made up my mind. Maybe it was a little of my heart ruling my head and the thought of wearing that blue jersey. I hadn't enjoyed my trial there as much as I had at Chester, but there was something about Everton the others didn't have. I found the people different. They can be a little cocky, but I got on well with them and they seemed to accept me more than at the other clubs. Mind you, Dad would not have let me go anywhere, even to his beloved Everton, to sign schoolboy at fourteen unless I was guaranteed an apprenticeship at the end of it. He didn't want me slung away after a couple of years like some clubs do. His dad had done the same for him and it was a good move for me. Dad was chuffed because he wanted the best for me. Mum? I think she was pleased but her reaction was more low key. She's a down-to-earth lady who would rather go shopping for tights in Chester than watch Everton, son or no son.

3

The Big Climb

I remember the day I first left home – getting on the train, Mum and Dad waving, moving into digs. But it wasn't exactly tearful Tom Brown schooldays stuff. I knew I'd be back every weekend. And I was only twenty miles away. In fact, the best part of the whole thing for me was getting away from home. Not because I didn't love being there, but I was sixteen, an age when you want to do your own thing. I quickly found that things change as soon as you cross that boundary between schoolboy and apprentice. They're as nice as pie until they get your name on that form. Then it's different. The swearing starts which is something you never heard when you were signed as a schoolboy. Suddenly the orders are sharper. But I adapted. If you don't, you're out on your backside.

It is the time when the hard work starts – the eighteen months to two years that form the most important part of your football career. That's when strength and stamina are built up as well as technique. For some, that period is harder than others. Looking at Stevie McMahon bossing Liverpool's midfield, you may find it hard to believe that he was once an eight-stone weakling. In fact, Everton kept him on amateur forms another two months before giving him his apprenticeship. Now he's almost the same weight as me, thirteen stone.

It was the distance running that used to get to me. The sprints were no bother but when it came to the other stuff I must be a little bit in front of Bobby Mimms and a little behind Graeme Sharp. I just could not do their twelve-minute runs to save my life. But in the end, I was doing them twice a day!

Coach, Colin Harvey, set the standard. If you didn't finish in front of him, you had to do it again. There would always be a couple looking behind to see where Colin was and he'd be shouting, 'Don't worry, I'm still here!' The thing with me was that I always had him in my sights, dodgy hips and all, because he was always in front of me. And if I did edge ahead I'd still have to look out. If there were ten seconds left, he'd sprint ahead of you and then shout, 'Time. You, you and you do it again this afternoon.' He was a hard man. It got so that I couldn't sleep on Monday nights, knowing what Tuesday meant. One of those days I shall remember as long as I have muscles to ache. By that time, I was a pro and had a car. On the way in, a tyre punctured about one and a half miles from the training ground. I was late as it was and panicking about that twelve-minute run, so I pulled into a side street and ran to work. When I got there I was absolutely knackered. But the first thing I heard was 'top corner' which meant the run. Well, I must have finished half a pitch behind the rest. So Colin said, 'You're doing it again after training.' I did and finished behind them again. So it was, 'You're doing it again in the afternoon.' I did it three times that day. What with those and my run from the car, I was exhausted. But that was Colin. He would push and push you. OK, I was never going to be a long-distance man, but I needed that pushing and I think I earned some respect from him for keeping at it. Nowadays, they accept I'm not going to be a threat to Said Aouita, but they don't let me skive off either. All they ask is that I keep up.

I keep thanking my stars that I had Colin as my first coach.

He never stopped trying to improve me, even if I was not always willing. He called me back in the afternoons for extra sessions when I could have been playing snooker. Mostly it was for functional work – forwards against the back four. At times, it was boring. And I felt the exercise was more for the forwards than defenders, but all the while, without realizing it, you were picking up more about the way plays could be built up against you and how you could cope with them. I never moaned – at least not out loud – but I know how good that work was for me. Colin also used to go mad at me about my tackling. He wanted me to be meaner. He'd say scornfully, 'You, you'd go through a season without being booked. You've got to get into the habit as a centre-half of letting people know you're there. If your man's being a bit naughty, be a little bit naughty back.' And he would make his point painfully, getting off his feet to make tackles on me that rattled my teeth. I'd look down and think 'you . . .!' and then realize the guy who was doing this was probably causing himself more physical problems by making the point to the pupil the best way he knew. It was a hard lesson, but all he was trying to say was that it was a battle out there and what he was demanding of me was part and parcel of the professional game. If you're a big softy, you're not going to last two minutes. You're going to be a walkover for any hard, fit rival who isn't always going to stick to the gentleman's code. It didn't come naturally, but I think there will be a few strikers round the circuit who will reckon Colin did his job well.

There are three main levels of player at a football club – apprentices, young pros and the first teamers – with a kind of class barrier keeping them apart. You don't really have much to do with anyone in the other two groups. The nearest thing to an exception is the apprentice. One of his jobs is getting the first team's kit ready and it's then sometimes that he finds another hidden side to the star's nature. Paul Lodge certainly did – the hard way! Generally, the apprentices were wary of Bruce Rioch. The Scotland skipper was aggressive. If he said something, you jumped – fast. One day, Paul made the mistake of laying out Rioch's kit wet. The result was that he was pinned to a wall like some knife-thrower's assistant while footballs were hammered at him. And Bruce had a helluva shot. Paul finally emerged from the barrage shaken and wiser. You can bet Bruce's kit was drier than the Sahara after that. I might have thought about trying it now except the lads would know they were in no danger I'd hit them! Bob Latchford was the opposite to Rioch. The gentle hitman, Everton's top post-war goalscorer, had a very slow fuse. If you lit it, watch out. But we never saw that side of him. The niceness of the man showed itself once when we were late getting the kit ready. Latchy, who always seemed to be first in, could have given us a mouthful and waited. But no, he just mucked in and helped us sort it out. That was a big gesture from an England international.

Mike Pejic is another who never thought himself too big to help an apprentice. In fact, he went out of his way. The left-back was a great player and a fantastic bloke although not a great mixer with the lads. He was a loner. Not one of those who would go out for a drink and a good time. And footballers like people to muck in. It makes them feel more together. Pejic felt more at home with Dave 'Tizer' Thomas, the little winger who worked so well with Latchy. Tizer was another individualist. He preferred his garden to socializing. In fact, he was so keen with the green fingers, he wouldn't let the kids in there! Whatever others felt, for me Pejjy could do no wrong, on or off the field. I used to travel with him every day after he had taken Kevin Keegan's old farmhouse not far from us. He used those shared journeys to pass on the defender's tricks of the trade, telling me what to do in certain situations and how to cope with certain players. Maybe he didn't realize the effect those chats had on a young player. But I tried to remember everything. It was tragic he had to quit the game early because of terrible pelvic trouble, and it is good to hear he is back in the league coaching Port Vale. Those lads have a great, understanding teacher. He even had a nose job to celebrate! When he was at Goodison I hadn't seen a flatter hooter on anyone apart from Charlie Magri. Now it's more like Alan Minter's.

Pejjy also helped show my mate, Jakey, that footballers aren't some kind of untouchables from outer space. I have been mates with Jakey since I was five years old. And the friendship hasn't changed because I've got a bit more money while he's often looking for a job. Around my home area, it's a sticky time for employment for eighteen-twenty-year-olds. There's a lot of people who don't seem to trust that age group. Anyway, I admire Jakey because he never lets it get him down. He always believes something will turn up and he'll go round knocking on factory doors until someone gives him the right answer. But when it came to footballers, he was starry eyed. I didn't count because he'd grown up with me. Anyway, I was a young pro who wasn't in the team. Well, Pejjy went some way to clearing his mind. It happened that Pejjy heard my nan could get salmon and asked if he could have some. When I was going to deliver it, I asked Jakey if he wanted to go, too. Jakey couldn't get over the thought that he was going to an England player's home. Then he met Pejjy and realized what an ordinary bloke he was. We were there two and a half hours chatting, drinking, playing snooker with his kids. When we came out, Jakey said, 'I can't believe it. He's just like me and you!'

Not until then did I realize that people do put footballers on a different level; which is wrong. Maybe we can go out a little more and not worry about the cost of a meal, or where to get the money for a shirt. Other than that, and the job we do, we are just ordinary men. I must admit that it does hit me sometimes that while I have a tremendous job and good money there'll be mates who are out of work and struggling. It did bother me that it might affect friendships. But I needn't have worried. I've still got the same friends I had at school. If anything, people who didn't want to talk to me at school have suddenly changed. But they are the kind who only want to talk about football. If they get on that line, I'll turn it round and ask them what they do for eight hours a day and they soon shut up. My real mates never harp on about it.

I know it's easy to say it, but money is not the be-all or end-all for us. My wife, Sharon, would rather we lived in a council house if it meant everybody was happier. Fame is something we tolerate more than welcome. I've never used it to get a restaurant seat. And I've had less in the way of perks than many might think. One of the nicest things I've had was a gold sovereign from a local tailor, Ted Jones, who is an Everton fan and shareholder. I had it mounted on a chain and was bitterly disappointed when it was stolen in a burglary. If there's anything I resent about fame it would be the loss of privacy. It can get embarrassing, especially when I'm out with Sharon and the kids, Caroline and Dean. But it's one of the things we have to live with. I guess there would be more than a few who would risk fame to swap lifestyles with me.

4

The Four Musketeers

When Billy Bingham was sacked as boss at Goodison in 1977, I was on schoolboy forms and just about the only connection I had with him was watching the apprentices clean off the training ground walls the 'Bingham must go' graffiti. His successor, Gordon Lee, was six months into his spell when I got my apprenticeship. I didn't really know him either. I don't think anybody did. But he was a man who had a bit of the Basil Fawlty about him. He attracted accidents. Typical was the day I stormed into his office, ready to rip his head off when he hadn't even named me in his squad. But all the flak I was saving up ready to let loose was gone the moment I walked in. He swung himself backwards in his chair and gave his head a thump on a cupboard. He must have hurt himself, but he tried to act as if nothing had happened. 'Can I help you?' he asked. I just cracked up inside. 'You need to help yourself, mate,' I thought and completely lost the mood for a blazing argument. Gordon suffered something similar in Rotterdam. Feyenoord have a folding roof to their tunnel and he walked out just as it was coming down. He sat through the first half with blood trickling down that great dome of a head.

Yes, Gordon was capable of some funny things. Ask George

Wood. When a hotel door was broken on a foreign trip, he was fined and the big keeper wasn't even with the party. I think it was habit. If there was a bit of trouble in those days, it was George who got the blame. But Gordon was a likeable fella. I'll always have a soft spot for the man who gave me my first-team chance. And he didn't do a bad job for Everton for a while. The season he took over, only two of the last eighteen league games were lost and we reached the League Cup final and FA Cup semi-final. In his first full season, Everton were third and the First Division's highest scorers. Gordon's troubles started when Steve Burtenshaw, who had been Bingham's number two, left to manage Sheffield Wednesday. The pair had worked wonders. Steve could put things over well and the lads liked him. But he was ambitious and Gordon couldn't do much about that. Eric Harrison, who was promoted from reserve team coach, was different. In fact, he was two vastly different characters – great to know off the pitch and a bawling tyrant in the dug-out. I know what I'd say if he tried it on now, but at that time he left me petrified to have the ball. You knew if you did something wrong that first your eardrums and then your confidence would suffer. There was not much that was constructive about his flak. It got to the stage where I was happier playing in the reserves under Colin. Eric's was a sergeant-major approach which might have been effective with the kids but needed to be adapted when dealing with seasoned professionals. Unlike Colin Harvey, he could not change. There was a troubled pre-season tour of Germany and within three months Dave Thomas and the equally unhappy Colin Todd had been transferred. Latchy was soured but stuck it out. That was the start of a disastrous season in which we were near relegation and failed in an FA Cup semi-final.

It was still a big year for me – the breakthrough I had dreamed about and worked for. I knew I was on the first-team fringe, and I was ready. I didn't want to wait much longer. I was still determined not to stay if Everton felt I didn't have enough to offer the first team at nineteen or twenty. My contract was up in the summer and that was my deadline. But I did begin to be picked for the squad. And it was great for me just to go away with players I wasn't even training with at that time. My first away trip was at Norwich and memorable for daft reasons. Room-mate, Peter Eastoe, woke me so urgently on the Saturday that I thought the place was on fire. No, he'd just become a dad, had forgotten to send his wife flowers and could he borrow a fiver to put it right. Then I found the pants of my best suit, worn specially for the occasion, had accidentally got soaked with water – I was still trying to get them dry by the time we got on the coach.

Peter may not have been so good at remembering his wife at the odd birth, but he was great the way he looked after rookie Ratcliffe. He was as terrific a character as he was a player. All he lacked to be special on the pitch was a bit of pace. He reminded me of Dalglish the way he shielded the ball and held it up while others got in position. The crowd didn't give him credit for what he did but any player who figured in the same side will tell you how good he was.

My big chance finally came right out of the blue in March – at Manchester United. I just had time to phone Dad and he made it to the game with Uncle Graham and Paul. I was in because John Gidman had been hit by a virus. I think Gordon Lee knew all day that he would play me but didn't say anything so I could have a good afternoon's 'kip' before the game. I didn't even realize Giddy had a virus until I came down for the pre-match meal. Then Mick Lyons said casually, 'I think you're playing. Giddy's not fit.' That's the way it was. Billy Wright switched to right-back with me in the centre.

It was a big game for the team as well as for me. We needed points. Everton were nineteenth and hadn't won in six games. United were second that year under Dave Sexton. I was playing alongside Lyonsy against Joe Jordan and Lou Macari. I couldn't have had anybody better to be with than Mick in my debut. The big man went for everything in the air and I just cleaned up behind him. Jordan was known for his tremendous aggression but he tried nothing nasty on the kid in front of him. I can't remember even a snarl. In fact, my adrenalin was flowing so fast I would not have felt it if he'd hit me with a steamroller. It also helped settle me when I got in a good forty-yard pass for Brian Kidd early on. The only other thing that struck me about that night was the fantastic roar when Jimmy Greenhoff got off the subs' bench. I suddenly heard this staccato 'Green-hoff, Green-hoff' chant taken up by the United hordes. I don't know about him but it wound me up. And he didn't make much impact when he came on for the struggling Macari. We drew 0–0 and I was happy with what I'd done. More important everyone else seemed to be. I even got a smile from my United fan, Grandad, who was usually only happy if the reds were rampant.

There wasn't much time to savour it. Giddy was fit and back for the next game and I was back in the reserves. But the next call wasn't far away – for the FA Cup semi-final replay with West Ham at Leeds. I didn't even know I was in the reckoning. I was playing in the reserves when the first game was drawn, 1–1, at Villa Park. But there was a vacancy because Brian Kidd had been sent off and so was out of the replay. Joe McBride, the Scottish under-21 forward, was rooming with me at the team hotel and I thought if one of us was going to play it would be him. The way we found out who was lucky was typical Gordon Lee. As we headed for the lift, Gordon stepped out, then while we were getting in and the doors were closing, he suddenly said to me, 'You're playing.' And to Joey, 'You're not.' It was just another example of how he always seemed to be thinking about something else.

I enjoyed everything about the night but the result – a 2–1 loss in extra time to a freak header from right-back Frank Lampard. Peter Eastoe and Mick Lyons slumped in the dressing-room, not ashamed to cry. Like Latchy, who didn't openly show his grief, they knew at their age it would almost certainly be their last chance of an FA Cup final. That was what they kept repeating and they were right. I felt almost guilty at not feeling more than disappointed. But then I had another ten years. I was sorry for Joe McBride, too. His parents had come down to watch and he was really in the doldrums. But nobody could afford to feel sorry for himself for long. Everton still needed points and the next game was at Tottenham. I stayed in for that and then got a helluva shock. We were beaten 3–0 and Gordon laid into everybody individually, apart from keeper Martin Hodge, Eastoe and me. I didn't know whether I'd escaped the blow-out because I hadn't played too badly or because I was young. Then, a week later, we were in a Southport hotel the night before the home game with Southampton and it came up on TV that Everton had dropped three players. I just had time to say to room-mate Hodgey, 'wonder who they are', when my name came up. I was amazed considering that I hadn't been criticized, and hurt that I had to learn on TV that I was dropped. It also angered me that Gordon hadn't the decency to tell me. But Gordon was unpredictable. I wasn't even in the squad for the next game and it provoked me into making my first of many trips to the manager's door to find out why.

Just as I was feeling low, someone came along to lift me – Mike England. He named me as one of four lads wanted on stand-by for Wales' British championship squad. It was Ian Rush's call-up, too. At first, all I had to do was keep fit in case anyone collapsed. Then, when David Jones was injured in the 4–1 beating of England at Wrexham, the call came while I was taking Sharon out. Dad was waiting for me when we got back and told me I was wanted in Glasgow, fast. I was on the next train. I got no nearer the action against Scotland than the subs' bench but it was another step up. I know in those days it seemed you only had to go there on holiday to get a cap but it was special to me. Just being in that squad makes you feel better. You seem to do things in training you wouldn't previously do or try. Your confidence is raised. It just gives you something else to fight for because you want to keep being part of it.

I was scared stiff going up to Scotland that first time. Here I was, just three games under my belt, about to mix with people like Joey Jones who had been my idol. I needn't have worried. I felt more welcome in that squad than in Everton's first team. But that was through circumstances more than anything. I didn't muck about with Latchy and co, or drink with them. I just worked with them and that was it. I knew Rushy, Peter Nicholas and Jeremy Charles from my youth team days and there was a young element in the Welsh squad. But it wasn't just a case of three or four going out together, but everyone. That was important for a newcomer, especially one more used to reserve football. It was more like a football club than an international side.

Joey Jones and Mickey Thomas were particularly great at helping me ease in. Joey had every right to act the big star with me but he just treated me like a good neighbour, friendly and natural. Mickey just buzzes everywhere with endless energy – a sixteen-year-old wrapped up in a thirty-year-old body. Some can't see eye to eye with him but he couldn't do enough for me and we took to each other straight away. So we became like the Four Musketeers – Joey, Rushy, Mickey and me. Don't ask me who was D'Artagnan! Rushy and me roomed together and the other two paired off. After a while, as the friendship grew stronger, Mike England would make sure our rooms were kept well apart or there would be more than the usual mayhem! One night we wrecked their beds just for the hell of it and then we had to watch out. We'd gone a shade too far. Joey was not happy and when he had his serious look on you knew you had to watch it. The trouble was he'd just had the worst haircut you ever saw and though he was swearing and mad, all we could take in was this talking toothbrush! Anyway, as far as he was concerned, this was not the proper order of things. He told us that he was the one who gave out the stick in that squad, not a couple of upstarts. But he could never be serious long and he was great for defusing tension. There's no better example of that than before a tough 1981 World Cup qualifier in Turkey. That match came just after I'd been sent off against Manchester City. It was in the days when I was a bit of a hothead. The Turks latched on to this. They tried to put Byron Stevenson and me in the same category of public enemies. Why Byron? Well, in a previous match with the Turks he had punched a guy, broken his jaw and finished up being banned for three years. The management tried to keep the media away from me but I was pretty tense while waiting at Istanbul for the connecting flight to Ankara. Anyway, TV grabbed us for individual predictions about the result. So it went something like, 'this is Ian Walsh, Crystal Palace, 1–0 for Wales; Peter Nicholas, Arsenal, 2–0 for Wales. . .' When it got to Joey, he wound up saying, 'and this is Joey Jones, Istanbul airport, News at Ten!' Well, you should have seen the TV guys' faces. We were curled up but they were definitely not amused. In fact, they went up the wall. There were pointing fingers with an 'I'll have you outside' conversation. But the diversion had done the trick and eased the pressure on the lads. Joey was also into Cannon and Ball at the time so it was 'Rock on Tommy' every two minutes and exaggerated pretend butts at the backs of people's heads. When they turned round, he'd have the most fantastic straight face. He also did great imitations of comics John Cleese and Michael Barrymore.

To me, Joey is more important than a £1 million player to some teams because of his dressing-room banter. He and Mickey were a double act. Mickey was just as bad. A nutter. He used to have award nights. He was in his element if he could get on a stage or grab a microphone. He'd go through an Oscar ceremony routine and you had to fall in with the act or else! He caught Rushy beautifully one day, pretending he was a reporter. Mickey phoned him from next door to the hotel dining room, asked a few questions, then after a while said, 'Hold on, I've got a call on the other line.' At that point, he appeared through the dining room door and asked, 'Who're you talking to, Rushy?' Then he disappeared back to his booth and kept Rushy at it for a long time. I'm not sure he ever knew it was Mickey. Mad, completely mad. And, as a driver, he was frightening.

The North Wales contingent used to go in a three-car convoy to squad meetings. Besides the musketeers, there would be Dai Davies, Neville Southall and sometimes Dave Felgate. Now you might think, after his other antics, Joey would be a daft driver. Far from it. He's so safety conscious it's untrue. He doesn't believe in going over 60mph and if there was a 40mph limited, you can bet he'd be doing thirty-nine. We pointed out that the indicators were more than for telling others which way he was heading. They were also for OVERTAKING, but he wouldn't have it. But Mickey did stay in character when he got behind the wheel. He used to fly in and out the traffic in his 2.8 injection Capri. So what with Joey's caution and Mickey's grand prix style, our intended convoy ended up like one of those tortoise *v* hare cartoon races.

There's no way we could keep up with Mickey. He'd disappear over the horizon. Then we'd go round a corner and there he'd be, like Bugs Bunny, lying on the bonnet, sunbathing and snoring! As soon as we'd gone past, he'd be whizzing off past us again. Another five miles, another lay-by and Mickey would be there, polishing the car. By this time, we'd be crying with laughter. This used to go on until he ran out of ideas or tired of the game. He wasn't the only one who played tricks in cars. I once caught Rushy on another of our drives. It could have been the end of £3million worth of superstar, plus whatever Joey and I were worth. Jeremy Charles was behind us in Alan Curtis's car when suddenly their sunroof opened and Jeremy was throwing sweets at us. We weren't taking that. So I said to Rushy, 'Right, don't let them get away with it! Start firing back.' So he started to get up through my automatic sunroof and just as he was getting his aim I closed it. The effect was like one of those Jack in the Boxes being squashed back in his box, and he didn't like it. Joey and I couldn't stop laughing and that got him mad. The next thing he's wrenched at the steering wheel and I went straight across the road. Luckily nothing was coming or this confession would never have seen the light of day.

Do you remember the Terry Scott radio character? The horrible kid who'd say about his best mate 'he's my best friend and I hate him'? That's just about the way it is with me and Rushy. We're from the same area. We know the same people. We've been close for years. Drinking pals. Room-mates with Wales. I think the world of him – off the field! But on it he's been a pain to me; too many times the difference between Everton and Liverpool. And, for that part of our relationship, I was mighty glad to see the back of him when he went to Juventus. When we played against each other our friendship was left outside the ground. In his early days he wasn't physical and I used to make that work for me. But he learned. He got harder. It got to be a thing between us that I'd whack him and he'd try to whack me.

We nearly had a punch-up right in front of the royal box at Wembley. That was in the 1986 Charity Shield. Memories of losing out to Liverpool in the double a few months before were still too painfully fresh for us to feel much charity that day. Early on, I clattered Rushy hard from behind to let him know it was business as usual. He turned right round with fists up and eyes blazing. He knew it was me but he was annoyed and you couldn't blame him. Jan Molby came over and I looked at him as if to say 'keep off, this is nothing to do with you. This is a fight between friends.' In the end, Rushy held back, but if he'd wanted to fight me on the day I'd have taken him. Why not?

That's football. You're so wound up in it, you'll do anything not to lose – even clout your mate if you have to. Anyway, he had the last word, as he had a habit of doing, equalizing three minutes from time and denying us full possession of the shield.

There was another match when we clashed. I'd whacked him as he went for a ball and he came right back with his elbow across my nose. It started bleeding. I didn't want to go off so I was sniffling up the blood and blowing it out. The next minute, it got caught in my throat and I was choking to death on the halfway line. While I was doubled up in pain, I caught sight of him and he was laughing his head off! When I came round, I swore at him and said 'See what you've done. You nearly killed me.' But we finished up laughing. And that's the way it's been between us.

Once Rushy had learned to cope with the physical side there was not a lot, apart from pray, a defender could do against him to keep him quiet. He's the best finisher I've seen. And he seemed to relish playing against us. The fact he equalled Dixie Dean's Mersey derby scoring record says everything about his finishing. Our style of defence, holding a flat line at the back, just seemed to suit both him and Liverpool, the way they liked to thread balls through to him. And he is so quick I've seen him shock players by catching balls on the by-line they had been certain would go out.

There will be some who will wonder why, with his record against us, we never made special plans for him, putting a marker on him or playing a sweeper. Howard Kendall wouldn't do either and I went along with his reasoning. For a start, he did not want to make him a bigger bogey man to us than he was. And for another, Kendall refused to mess around with a system that had helped make us the best team in England. If you changed it for one man, you were casting doubt on its efficiency. All he ever said about Rushy was to be aware of him. I think you could say we were; but being aware of him and stopping him are very different things. The fact is we didn't think we played him too badly. He never had that many chances but every one he did get he seemed to put away. That's what makes him different from ordinary mortals. And he's just getting better and better. He waits to see what the keeper does and then puts the ball exactly where he doesn't want it. It doesn't matter who the keeper is, or what his reputation. You only have to remember what he's done against Neville Southall. Rushy's just in a different class. Clive Allen is a great finisher, but he's got a long way to go before you can put him on Rushy's level.

If his finishing and speed aren't enough to frighten you, there are other, less obvious, parts of his game which make him one of the best players I've played against or with. People don't realize all the work he puts into the game. And I've never admired him more for that than in his last season with Liverpool. With that £3million move to Juventus hanging over him, and the chance of one bad injury wrecking it, there would have been understanding within the game if he had slackened off a bit. He never did. In fact, it seemed a matter of pride that he did exactly the opposite. He really wanted to leave the fans something to remember him by – as if he hadn't already – and he was really sick when he didn't do it. That was true character. His passing has improved every year. The way he picks people out can be brilliant. Then there's his ability to defend better than any striker I've seen since Bob Latchford. That starts as soon as he loses the ball. He'll make defenders go the way he wants them to go and then sprint at them. Often, he'll panic them into giving a bad pass. And that sprint is no idle threat. Most strikers will put on a show of getting the ball back. Usually, it's bluff. They'll pull out at the last minute. But he won't. Defenders forget how quick he is – I know, because he's caught me – or just don't believe he'll go through with the challenge. But he does and he rarely gets beaten when he dives in.

If that's not enough, there's also a touch of the clairvoyant about him. He's a lot brighter than people think. And that football brain is so clever. A classic instance came when he scored the goal that equalled Dixie's record at Anfield at the back end of the 1986/7 season. When the cross came over from the left, I was probably favourite to get it and went for it. I didn't make contact. Rushy did and he had not gone with me as most would have done. All he did was wait for me to miss. And there he was in front of the net with the ball at his feet and we were done again! Lethal. He said to me later, 'As soon as the ball came over, I knew you weren't going to get it.' That's what I mean about clairvoyant. He just knows when people are going to make a mistake and he's ready. I've also seen him do something in matches I see no other centre-forward do – drop off away from an opponent if he knows he's not going to win a header and then go for the ball when it drops. He has the knack of knowing where that ball will drop.

It seems strange to think back now but it was a long time before I saw anything special about Rushy, or even became friends with him. We were from the same patch and there was only a year between us, but I didn't meet him until we played together in an under-thirteens semi-final down in Swansea. He was on the left wing and I wasn't very impressed. We'd only heard of each other before that. The truth is that I knew more about his brother, Stephen, than him. 'Step' was two years older and had set scoring records – which Ian promptly broke. Even so, I didn't see much to him. He was just a scrawny, scruffy little lad, and very thin. But he was known for being quick and a goal getter. I used to see him around Chester occasionally, maybe watching a game, and we'd say 'hello', but that was about all. As kids, we even used to train at Chester on different evenings, so we never came across each other there. And that didn't change until years later when we were in the full Welsh squad at Hampden in 1980.

I suppose it was natural then that two raw, inexperienced lads from Flint, a bit in awe of the big names, should drift together. And it was only then that we really started talking to each other and found we had so much in common. Everybody knows everybody else in Flint, or knows of them. If he ever mentioned a name, I'd know who he was on about and vice versa. It may surprise people to know but we hardly talked about Everton or Liverpool and it has stayed that way. If we meet up, the conversation about our games will take up about five minutes. Then it will usually be about local football, pub football, local personalities. That's partly why we get on so well. There's little 'shop' talk. We started rooming together and sometimes I ran him to work when he was banned from driving. Then, because we were in the Welsh squad, we'd give each other lifts to the games. Our friendship just grew over the years. I'm only sorry it wasn't as mates at Everton. And it could have happened. He was an Evertonian, but they never came for him. Maybe it was because he was so thin. But, as a player, it was a long time before he made his mark with me.

One of the things I remember about that first time in Scotland was that he put on the worst warm-up performance I've ever seen when he was called up to go on as sub for Ian Walsh. It was his debut and I don't know if it was nerves, or being at Hampden, or what it was, but he just seemed paralysed on the running track. He did absolutely nothing to warm up. Just stood there. I was on the bench and shouted, trying to get him going, but he still did nothing. Maybe it shouldn't have been surprising. He was only nineteen and very shy. Liverpool had paid £300,000 for him, but his confidence was low. He was struggling to break through at Anfield, surrounded by big names. Kevin Sheedy tells me that when Rushy was in the reserves he was hopeless. His touch was awful. Certainly, when I played against him in the mini derbies, he gave us no trouble. It was Sheeds, pinging the ball all over the place with that left foot, and Howie Gayle, with his terrific pace, who stood out. It was the same for Wales.

We'd have to practise free kick routines over and over again because his control kept letting him down.

He was so fed up at Liverpool he went in to see Bob Paisley about getting away. But Paisley wasn't having any of that. He'd seen something in Rushy and he wasn't going to let it go. It wasn't the worst decision the wise old man ever did for Liverpool! Everything changed for Rushy in one match – the 1981 League Cup final replay with West Ham. It's not often I want Liverpool to win a match but I did in that one. It was his big break and I wanted him to take it. Take it? He was sensational. I respect Billy Bonds, but he was made to look ultra slow in that game. And Rushy's touch, which had only been suspect, was fantastic. I couldn't believe it was the same lad. That was the first time I realized that he was special. And that match gave him the confidence to know he could live in that company and he's just gone on and on from there. I'll always remember his face when he picked up his medal. It was a picture. He didn't come round and show it to me. He'd have been slung out the door if he had. Friendship doesn't stretch that far! Anyway, he's not the kind of lad to go showing off. But we're always teasing each other about what we've won. At one time, I could beat him with my FA Cup medal. Now he can match that. He always used to hit me with the European Cup medals, but I'd get him over the number of caps I've got. It was just good banter. His success never strained our relationship. In fact, I was upset for him when local politician, Derek Hatton, got him angry after our derby win at Anfield in 1986 which we thought had virtually clinched the title.

I was in the car with Rushy and Tracey, then his girl friend, ready to pull out when a door opened and Hatton, an Evertonian, reached round the back, shook my hand and said, 'Well done, Rats.' Then he looked over at Rushy and said, 'Unlucky, Rushy! Wish I could say the same for you, today.' It may sound trivial but it was so insensitive. You can do without that when you've just lost a derby, especially what could have been a crucial one like that. It was embarrassing for me and Rushy was fuming. But he has learned the hard side of public relations as well. Early on, he made the mistake of talking too freely with people and got stung occasionally. Now he susses people out before he opens up. Remember, he's just an ordinary lad from an ordinary background. Public relations isn't part of that scene and he's getting pestered every minute of the day for one thing or another. He usually handles it with great good nature. But he only takes so much hassle and I wouldn't like to be on the wrong side of him. The Italians may yet find that out.

5

Howard's Way

If the 1979/80 season was one of tremendous advance for me, the next was to be utterly frustrating, even if it did include my first cap. And it wasn't only tough for me. It was to be the last of Gordon Lee's four years. There was a spell of six successive wins, starting in September, which pulled the club up to third in the First Division. But we won only six more during the rest of the season and went through March losing five in a row, scoring just once. That spelled the end for Gordon. We all had our problems. Mine was a running battle with John Bailey for a spot at left-back, a place that was only just better than nothing to me, but was the only one open.

Bails is in the Mickey Thomas–Joey Jones mould; the team joker and vital for team morale. Being a scouser, he's a natural comic. He'd have you falling about with ridiculous sayings like 'as quick as a leper' or 'happy as a log'. He would boast about his England B cap being 'worth eighty of your Welsh caps any day'. And he was appalled when Nev Southall, retaliating, wore in training the England jersey given him by Peter Shilton in a swap. But Bails was hard to put off. 'I remember when I played in the B team,' he'd drone on, 'and there's me and Big C, Cyrille Regis, standing there for the national anthem.' He'd then start humming the United States' *Stars and Stripes!* And he was serious! But when we were having our personal battle I did not find him very funny at all. In fact, it was the reverse. In training, if I got a chance to kick him, I kicked him. We'd argue over the slightest thing and it was mainly me who caused the aggro. He was older and more experienced and could take most of it with a pinch of salt.

We were also totally different types. I thought he was a bit flash. I was a defender who got stuck in and didn't feel too comfortable getting the ball from the keeper. Bails wasn't a good defender, although he improved when Howard came, but he was very good on the ball, full of confidence and tricks, and good at getting forward. It also didn't help our relationship that he was the favourite of the crowd who were on my back. So I was in and out the team and getting more and more fed up with the situation. Sharon got so used to taking my 'bad news' Friday phone calls her first words would be 'you're dropped, are you?' I'd take off to drown my sorrows. The only thing that lightened that gloom was one magic day, 19th November 1980, just a week after my twentieth birthday, when I got that first cap, in a World Cup qualifier against Czechoslovakia in Cardiff. Joey Jones gave me the hint when I rang about our usual lift operation. He wasn't going because of a damaged ankle and said, 'I think you'll be playing. All the best.' I was – against Marian Masny!

Maybe it's as well that name meant nothing to me at the time. I couldn't even pronouce it. But the media got very excited about the lad from Everton reserves facing this world class winger who'd apparently terrorized England in the European Championship not long before. Even some of the lads were whispering about this bloke. All Mike England said to me was, 'He's quick, but you're quick so you should be able to handle him.' I was quite nervous, but it was a tremendous help having a workhorse like Mickey Thomas in front of me to help out. I got in a good tackle on Mr Masny early on to show him I was around and then just enjoyed myself. I must have done all right because at half-time he switched wings. After all the build-up I was disappointed in him. He was nothing exceptional that night but the whole Welsh team were, with Leighton Phillips and Terry Yorath standing out. I didn't have long to savour it. It was soon back to reality and the reserves. But the cap did help make up for what was happening at Everton. I even felt different in training and the lads remarked on it. But at the back of my mind was always the thought that I was training only for reserve football and that made me feel very down. Silly, really. You know, despite everything, you're in the best job in the world. But. . .

It was at the beginning of the New Year that the team started sliding. There were rumours about Gordon going and Howard Kendall arriving. There was even talk of a straight swap, with Gordon going back to Blackburn. When that sort of rumour spreads, players worry about their future, especially if contracts are up. I didn't detect any change in Gordon, nor in Eric. The only noticeable differences were that there were fewer jokes flying about and training got harder, maybe as a punishment, which didn't help. We did so much running, I was feeling tired by Saturday. Silly goals were going in and things just got worse. Slight mistakes were penalized and the tension was showing. I wasn't playing well when I did get in at left-back. There were a few games at centre-back for me and it was then that I would feel happier and much more comfortable about my game. I just couldn't understand why the powers-that-be couldn't see that.

Gordon finally left in May. I first heard about it over the radio and straight away Howard was appointed. Neither announcements surprised the dressing-room. It had been common talk there. It seemed to me the board got rid of Gordon knowing Howard would come. I never even saw him to say 'goodbye'. The changeover happened before a testimonial at Anfield. Lyonsy, being skipper, went to see the new boss and was told that Eric was sacked, Mick Heaton would replace him, and that Colin Harvey and youth coach Graham Smith would stay. The boys were particularly pleased for Colin and Graham. Neither had done anything to get the bullet. Howard himself came in the dressing-room and just told us to 'go out and enjoy yourselves.' Little did we know just how enjoyable it would eventually be.

Howard Kendall kept his registration as a player and it was great for me to play alongside someone who I'd watched from the terraces in the 1970s. And he didn't make a bad first impression on me as boss. He called me in during the pre-season and told me that I was to have a rise. 'You're an international,' he said, 'and you should be paid a little more.' I had to sign for another year but this was a good start. Here, obviously, was a gaffer who thought more of me than the last one. I mean he had tried to sign me for Blackburn when Everton fancied Kevin Stonehouse.

How wrong I was. Ahead was the same old battle with Bails, and Sharon got her usual Friday call, only more often! But he came well briefed about the club and personalities and he was still influential as a player even if lasting ninety minutes was a problem. The pre-season training was brilliant. That annual month's slog for fitness is usually something to be dreaded, but Howard made it so interesting and different that you were coming in the next day actually looking forward to whatever it held.

Everything is done at the player's own pace. Gordon and Billy Bingham used to have the lads running up and down sand dunes at Ainsdale and injuries were caused through that. You'd be stiff as a board the day after one of those sessions. With Howard, if you felt stiff, all you had to do was tell him and he'd send you for a bath. It was emphasized that if we did go on a run, it wasn't a race. Previously, it had always been a race, either against rivals or the clock. Howard and Colin believe if you stretch in sprinting at that early stage of preparation, you're likely to pull a muscle. The ideas weren't unique. Howard had learned and borrowed them from Alan Durban at Stoke and put his own adaptation on them.

Everybody enjoyed the work and he got respect that way. He knew how a modern player thought; what he wanted and didn't want to do. He even, for the first time in my short experience, coached the back four into the way he wanted them to play. That involved working as a disciplined unit so that opponents ran offside in certain situations. It wasn't complicated but it took some getting used to. It was important during the learning process that the keeper should know everything about the system and that was a reason for him bringing Jim Arnold from Blackburn.

Howard's only early mistake in player relations was being too close to the lads. He tried to sit too much on our side of the fence. He used to go out for a drink and laugh and joke, which was great – up to a point. A manager must keep that little line of separation intact or his authority is at risk. Eventually, he realized this and cut down on the socializing.

Howard's first signings were his version of the Magnificent Seven – Mick Ferguson, Alan Biley, Alan Ainscow, Mickey Walsh, Neville Southall, Jim Arnold and Mickey Thomas. These were the best he said he could get for the money available. They all had their moments but only Nev and Arnie were successes, although Ains was very unlucky, breaking a leg at Notts County. Mickey Thomas would have been successful if he hadn't chosen to take on Howard. It was great for me to hear he was coming from Manchester United and he was chuffed to be with us. 'I've always been an Evertonian', he told us. He was a good left-sided player and could have done well for us. But I just don't know if Howard took to the lad who could not treat anything seriously.

Their blow-up happened after Mickey had played eleven games. He was injured, missed a few matches, and Howard wanted him to prove his fitness in the reserves at Newcastle before returning. Mickey argued he was fit and wanted to go straight back to the first team, just as Asa Hartford had. I'm not surprised he didn't fancy the trip. Newcastle isn't the best of places to go in the reserves. It's nearly always windy and raining and when there's no one watching it's desolate. I was in that match and when I heard he was playing, said to him, 'I'll see you here tomorrow.' No you won't,' he said. 'I'm not going. I'm not playing for the reserves.' And he wouldn't budge from that stand. I don't know whether Howard was making an early point to his players but the result was that Mickey was on his way out – fast. Mickey Walsh said that the lad was almost crying when Howard told him he could go and that Brighton wanted him. His Goodison career had lasted about three months. Howard's point, if that's what it was, was costly. We struggled down the left side after Mickey left.

Alan Biley was another to suffer the tough side of the boss. The blond striker gave the impression that he didn't have to work at the game. That attitude was always going to lead to confrontation. When we got beaten 1–0 at Arsenal, all hell broke around the poor lad's head. I've never heard a rollicking like the one Howard blasted into him. It was so bad Alan was crying on the coach journey home. He was utterly shocked. Howard told him he didn't want players who had no heart and who would not work and fight for their mates. He promised, 'If you can't do that, you'll never play for this club again.' The blast didn't work. To be fair, blood and guts just wasn't in Alan's game. Some players need always to be lifted, never flattened, and Alan played only a few more games. Alan Irvine, a clever Scottish right-winger, was another who needed the constant kid glove. Tell him he was the best in the world and he'd be a world beater for you. Slaughter him and he was lost to you.

Only Neville Southall is left of Howard's original Magnificent Seven, and that's fitting. Howard made some great signings after his first controversial splash out, but for me the big man was the best. The trouble with a goalkeeper is it's hard to say exactly what he's won you, but the fact that he was 1985 Footballer of the Year summed up how important he was, and is, to us. I'll give you a small example of how special he is. You won't see Everton conceding many penalties, if any, through tackles. And he's the reason. Defenders have such confidence in him they don't make desperate lunges on men who have still to beat Neville. Yet, when he arrived from Bury, we were in the same room and I didn't even know who he was. And he a Welshman. We didn't know much more for quite a while.

It took Nev a good year to settle. He felt like I did when joining up with Wales the first time, overwhelmed and out of place among the big names. I got on great with him, man to man. When we went away, he'd never shut up, but when he was with the lads he couldn't talk. There's no easier fella to get on with than Mick Heaton but he used to drive Nev to and from Bury every day and all he'd get in the way of conversation was 'morning' and 'thanks' and 'see you tomorrow'.

I've never seen so much of a change in a person as the one Nev went through. The key was the loan period he spent at Port Vale. It was the best thing that could have happened to him. This was a small club he could relate to and where he could feel at home. Nev's the rough diamond type you'll find in the scrapyard or bricky's yard. He felt at home with lads like Bob Newton who had had to learn the game down the League. By the time he returned, he had come out of himself and had come to terms with Everton. Within another year, he was asking about a rise and when Howard Kendall was explaining he couldn't give him one because he'd just bought Andy Gray and Terry Curran, the instant reply was, 'Well sell them then.' Now he's always taking the mickey, playing practical jokes. You've got to do that as a footballer – learn to join in the banter and give it back. If you don't, you'll live the rough, loner's part of the game.

Nev learned plenty from Jim Arnold, a very different sort in every way. Arnie appeared more like an accountant on the way to a convention than a player. He was tall, thin and looked too old. He also used to wear these odd suits and ties. Terry Curran took such a dislike to one particular tie that he threatened to cut it off if he wore it again. Jim did and out came Terry's scissors. But Arnie did ever so well for us. Nev was more of a stopper then, diving at your feet and spreading himself. Arnie would wait. He was a great reader of where people would put the ball and he'd be diving before the player put it there. At that time, he was doing everything right and keeping Nev out. But a lot of his game rubbed off on Nev, which is another reason the big man is so hard to beat.

They say keepers are one-offs and there's certainly nobody quite like Nev. I remember him turning up at Wembley once in suit and flip-flops. He did have bad feet, but he's the sort who would only dress in his tracksuit if he could get away with it. There's no side to him. When he was Footballer of the Year, it took all the gaffer's persuasion to get him to bring in the trophy for the next season's photocall. And how many people do you know have a sponsored car and can't drive? He has to be driven round by his wife.

He doesn't drink because he knows alcohol could balloon his bulk and yet he can still be the life and soul of the party. And he eats nothing but plain food – steak or chicken. Another unusual thing about him is that if he wasn't a keeper he could have earned a living doing a Dave Watson. A lot of keepers fancy themselves out of goal just as strikers fancy themselves in it, but Nev's one of the few who could actually do a different job. He's skilful, sometimes brilliant. He's also a workaholic. When he first came, he actually asked the gaffer if he could get him a part-time job labouring to fill his time when he wasn't training! And he's so fierce about his training that he gives managers nightmares. It doesn't matter what day it is, or what the ground's like, he'll throw himself at everything.

We try to wrap him in cotton wool on Fridays and send him

home, but he'll be in on Saturday, diving about with everybody wincing in case he does something to his fingers. I've never seen anybody work as hard as he does in kick-abouts. They're not warm-ups with him. His pride's at stake with every shot. The strain of it really told on Howard Kendall before the FA Cup tie at Stoke that started our 1985 Wembley run.

Nev had gone out early with Alan Harper and their session ended with a penalty contest. There were 10,000 Evertonians there loving it, roaring with each save. Howard heard all this noise, looked through the window and snapped, 'What're they doing? Why aren't they taking this seriously?' Their antics made everybody relax on a pretty tense occasion but when Nev got back, Howard said, 'What the hell are you doing, you big, soft Nelly?' Nev shrugged those massive shoulders and said, 'I'm only having a warm-up, aren't I?'

If Nev wasn't a workaholic he couldn't have got back so fast after his terrible ankle ligament injury which he picked up playing for Wales in Dublin back in March 1986. It was that, plus great medical care and luck that got him through. Funnily enough, I missed that match with ankle ligament damage myself, but I know Wales' team doctor, Dr Graham Jones, must take a lot of credit for the fact Nev's playing now. As soon as he fell awkwardly on that ankle, the doc got him into a splint and took him straight to hospital. The luck was that a top ankle specialist was on duty and did the operation immediately. There had been talk of Nev being flown straight home but the specialist said if he didn't operate there and then the ligaments would tangle, making the recovery period much longer. The specialist was so quick that by the time the match was over and the lads dressed, Nev was awake in his room. The next day, Littlewoods sent their private jet for him.

Howard took that injury badly. Here he was, within reach of the double and without the world's best keeper. As it happened, we had every confidence in Bobby Mimms and he kept six clean sheets in the last nine games. It wasn't his fault we missed out. But the day after the match when Mike England tried to soften the blow, saying 'it could have happened any time, even in training,' Howard snapped, 'No it couldn't. We don't train on Wednesdays.' He was annoyed that Nev had played although it wasn't a competitive match. But I think he might have had a different attitude if it had involved one of the England lads playing against Eire. He wouldn't have said 'no.' You always want to play for your country. Managers are on the other side. They try to do the best they can for themselves and you can't blame them. If I'm ever a manager I'll probably feel the same when it's my job on the line. Nev didn't talk a lot about that injury but I've never seen anybody work so hard to get back. He was playing by September when others might not have been active until Christmas – if at all.

6

Rucks with Howard

Howard may have been a breath of fresh air in many ways, but, when it came to the crunch, that air was as stale in my nose as it ever was. Our relationship rapidly cooled, rise or no rise. I was left out of the pre-season matches and it wasn't exactly unexpected when he pulled me aside before the First Division opener with Birmingham and said, 'I'm playing Bails.' I was still hurt, but all I said was, 'at least you've made your mind up before the day of the match.' Everton won 3–1 so I was resigned to another lengthy reserve stint. But three days later, I was in the team at Leeds. I don't know who was more shocked, Bails or me. It didn't last long. Our little see-saw was soon back in the old groove. Looking back, I can't believe I could go through a period like that. I'd play a few games, then he'd be back for a spell. Howard would call me in to tell me why. But the more it happened, the shorter our conversations were. 'You know what this is about?' he'd say. I'd come back, 'Yeah, it's not worth me staying to talk about it, is it?'

Sharon and I had only been married about a year and she must have wondered what she'd taken on. At that time, it was a grump who would start too many of her weekends by telling her he was off to drown his sorrows. Come to think of it, every weekend in the season must be a little hell to her. Even when I'm playing I'm not easy to live with near a game. As for Howard, I didn't like him. He came over as a nice, genuine fella, but I just couldn't hit it off with him. There was something about him that jarred with me. Maybe it was simply because I wasn't playing. Later, I came to like him and understand his ways. But at the time, I felt I was being used. When I was put in the side, it was not because of what I could do but only to give someone else a kick up the backside. I was worth more than that. I was also concerned how my situation at Everton would affect my rating with Wales. If you're not playing first-team football, you're not going to play international football. So when I wasn't picked to wear the red shirt it made me certain I had to get away. But the fact he kept bringing me back meant I held off taking that massive step.

The club didn't exactly set the place alight, finishing eighth, getting knocked out of the FA Cup at the first shout and the League Cup at the fourth. After all, Howard was still learning the ropes. He'd played in the First Division but coached and managed only in the Second, and that's a different ball game. Relationships generally were pretty good although I was down in the dumps. But everybody had their arguments with him and I was no exception. They were arguments you couldn't win, no matter how strong your case. Whether he felt that giving in was a sign of weakness I don't know, but that's the way it was.

For instance, he would tell me to hit the ball into the channels between players rather than to their feet. But that was pointless with Peter Eastoe up front. His strength was holding up the ball, not pace, and I argued that he was asking me to give Peter the wrong service. What did he say? 'I tell you what to do and if you don't do it, you don't play. And if he doesn't get on the end of the balls you hit in the channels, he doesn't play.' He also told me before a game with Manchester United to force Stevie Coppell inside. When I did and he scored, Howard made it my fault although I'd followed instructions.

At the turn of the year, Howard made his first big buy, going back to Stoke and paying £700,000 for Adrian Heath. It didn't work out so well at the start. We called him 'Howard's son' because he was so small and because that was the way Howard seemed to regard him. But for a long time he was more like a lost boy. He was only twenty-one, carrying a big money tag, and Goodison can be an intimidating place. He also suffered two break-ins almost before he'd got his luggage in the house. And on the field it didn't help that we didn't seem to know whether to play him up front or midfield. Stevie McMahon liked playing alongside him and reckoned his work and running were underestimated, but to me he didn't seem to know what he was doing in midfield. If he was going to make it, it would be up front and his later partnerships with Graeme Sharp and Andy Gray proved it. But it took him three years and much painful switching before it came right. It's fortunate he's a fella who doesn't show hurt. He has shown great resilience to survive and become such an important member of the squad that finally turned this club around.

The final straw for me came in November 1982 in the shape of poor Glenn Keeley. I say 'poor' because he has a unique place in Mersey football history that I wouldn't wish on anyone – a loan player sent off in his only game, a derby. How did he come to be put in that position? I never heard a reasonable explanation. There was no logic to it. The only thing he had going for him was a knowledge of Howard's system as one of his Blackburn old boys. I'd think twice before asking a £1million player to do what he was asked to do. Glenn, not the quickest player you ever saw, was thrown in straight from the Second Division, short of match practice because of injury, and asked to help Billy Wright stop Kenny Dalglish, then at the top of his crafty powers, and Ian Rush, whose pace would worry a cheetah.

It was a decision that left me dazed and angered. Ironically, Howard had just come to terms with the fact, which I thought was always blindingly obvious, that if I was going to make it, it would be at centre-back, not left-back. And I was geared up to play. Mark Higgins was injured and I thought my pace would be needed against Rushy. I also knew the way he played. Instead, I finished up fuming in the stand alongside Higgy and determined to get away. Glenn himself showed no doubt. The tall Londoner was full of himself – but he'd never experienced the pressures of a Mersey derby that can leave you exhausted before you've left the dressing-room. The result was one of the blackest days in Everton's history – and on our own turf! Liverpool won 5–0, Rushy scoring four and equalling a forty-seven-year-old derby-scoring record. Evertonians didn't know where to look. One lad was so uptight he was running up and down the steps in the stand, fists clenched and shouting, 'The bastards! The bastards! How can I go to work on Monday?' I didn't know if he was referring to Liverpool or us, but I understood. Glenn's contribution lasted thirty-seven minutes. He was sent off for hauling back Dalglish. A harsh victim of the new get-tough laws. I felt sorry for him, but sorrier for myself. I was giving Rushy a lift home and of course he arrived at the car park with the match ball signed by both teams. At least he didn't have my signature on it! Rushy's not the type to rub it in but I was so angry I nearly filled in one bloke who said when he saw him getting into my car, 'Why are you giving that redneck a lift?'

As far as I was concerned, it was the finish between me and Everton. I felt I was a better player than Glenn and yet here I was down to fourth or fifth in the pecking order. Next working day, I stormed into Howard's office and told him I'd had enough. 'I can see nothing for me here,' I said. 'I want to get away and I want the request put before the board.' I'll never forget his insulting reply. 'Who do you think would buy you?' he asked. That hurt but I said, 'Just put me on the list and we'll find out.' I never knew if he was right about my appeal. Managers let you know what they want you to know. It was only later I found out that Stoke had been interested and I could have been playing alongside Mickey Thomas again. But by the time I discovered that, things had changed completely for me. Within a month of that Liverpool fiasco, I had broken through at centre-back and at the annual spring PFA dinner Howard pulled me aside and said, 'Stoke have come in for you and I've told them where to get off! I'm offering you a new contract.'

There was no silver lining for Glenn Keeley. I never saw him again as a colleague. He was just allowed to drift quietly back to Blackburn without being given the courtesy of another chance to see what he could do in a more normal situation. If he was good enough in the first place, surely he was entitled to that? It looked like somebody was trying to pretend he never happened. But memories like that can't be wiped out and the after-effects of that defeat could have been disastrous.

If Howard's judgement was suspect there he had done brilliantly to snatch Kevin Sheedy from Liverpool, giving him the best left foot in the business and real quality down the left side. Sheeds is so lazy looking. He isn't the quickest player in the world. But he's special. Howard once brought in dance expert Len Heppell to help us improve movement. But, pointing to Sheeds, he said, 'You can take any player you like, except that one over there. Him you don't touch.' The gaffer thought if you speeded his game up he'd never be the same and that's the last thing he would risk. It makes me cry to think that Wales missed out on such talent. But he had Republic of Ireland qualifications too, and they moved quicker.

Bringing back Andy King and David Johnson was another matter. Kingy was a likeable, chirpy cockney and the best finisher I've ever seen – on the training field! He'd chip George Wood so often he'd make him mad and one of the sights in training was the big keeper chasing Kingy round the park like something out of Tom and Jerry. But I felt that his was a talent wasted. And his arrival only complicated Adrian Heath's difficult settling-in period. It was hard to accommodate both.

As for Jonno, everyone thought he'd do it at our place, but it turned out a nightmare, which his goal tally – four in thirty-five games – underlined. He didn't help himself by always saying we must do it the Liverpool way. That we shouldn't try difficult things. Someone pointed out, 'But Jonno, you're the one who's always giving it away.' I was sorry to see him struggle. He's a genuine fella maybe too nice – who would lend you £100 and not ask when he was getting it back. But nothing went right for him and he had argument after argument with Howard, usually over wanting to do things the Liverpool way, which was really not his business. At times, he seemed to be trying to take over and one American visitor actually thought he was a coach, he was directing so much. It didn't help that the crowd labelled him 'Liverpool reject' and booed his name when it was announced. But he'd just grin, wave and stoke them up some more. I remember when he came, Howard went on TV and said, 'If I was a defender, it would scare me to see Sharp and Johnson together.' Next day, a caller on Ian St John's phone-in radio programme replied with typical scouse humour, 'I don't know about them scaring the manager, they frighten the living daylights out of me!'

Certainly, they didn't frighten too many but nor did anybody else. After the Keeley episode, confidence inside the club was low. Nobody wanted the ball. Within a month we slipped from seventh to fifteenth, scoring one goal. I don't know what would have happened if Terry Curran hadn't come on loan in December. When that was announced, we looked at each other and asked, 'Why Terry? He's not the sort of player needed for this situation.' We wanted someone who could get stuck in and fight, not some Fancy Dan. We were utterly wrong. He was absolutely what we needed – a bubbly character who lifted the whole place. It didn't matter that he had come from Third Division Sheffield United. He had this terrific self-belief and his cockiness drew confidence from others, particularly the younger lads. The crowd loved him and pushed Howard to sign him so hard that he was embarrassed. He'd already spent £2million and money was tight. It was almost another year before Terry came full time but he never made the same impact. By that time, the crowd had turned on him because when Howard had tried to sign him a few months after his terrific spell he was turned down during negotiations with Terry's agent and reacted bitterly.

Howard didn't like agents. It was one of the reasons he fell out with Stevie McMahon and lost a player we could not afford to lose. All Stevie wanted was the same money as the other first teamers but Howard thought he was too young to have that money and banned the agent who had been advising him. Funnily enough, Howard soon got himself one of the Mr Ten Per Cents when he went off to Bilbao!

Nobody will know the extent of Howard's debt to Curran for that loan spell. From a position of not knowing where the next goal was coming from, we put together a run which took us to fifth before slipping a little. It was during that little run that Howard added another gem, Peter Reid, though it took a long time for the little motivator to convince the gaffer how good he was. In fact, there were times when he was in despair. I like to think I had something to do with the recovery, too. It was in the second game of Curran's spell that I was suddenly brought in to partner Mark Higgins at Ipswich.

Everton won for the first time in seven games and we stayed together in a great partnership, despite official doubts about having two left-footers together, until split by Higgy's terrible pelvic injury. I was helped in that game by Howard's tactics. He left out Kingy and stuck Kevin Richardson in front of our defence, telling him to cut out passes directed at Eric Gates, Paul Mariner and Alan Brazil. Richo did it well. Howard used to try little ploys like that but it was the first time I could remember one working. I didn't go into that game with any expectations, nor did I come out with any. The only reason I'd got in was because Billy Wright was overweight and dropped.

Again, I was only in to give someone else a gee-up, not on merit. I didn't like that, but it gave me my chance and from that day I've never really looked back. If it wasn't for Billy's problem, I don't think I'd have been playing today.

It was tough on him but you would have thought he would have taken more care. He only had to look at food to put on pounds. And he had been warned. When he weighed in at 13st 4lb on the Monday, he was told to 'do something about it'. He did. Three days later, he was 13st 8lb. He had been out for a meal to celebrate his wife's birthday and never dreamt that he would be weighed again so soon. When he got dropped, he lost 8lb straight away. Billy could lose it as quickly as he could put it on. Really, I went into that game playing to get away. I had no reason to think my situation had changed. I believed Billy would be back as soon as he'd got his weight right. For me, it was no more than a big chance to show anyone watching what I could do in a position where I was happy and comfortable. Maybe it was that attitude that helped. I'd come in at a bad time in the club's affairs and maybe it was because I thought I was going to get a transfer that I felt easier in my mind than the others. They were fighting for their places while I was nice and relaxed. There was anxiety in the place. I felt it but I was not going to let it get me down because I didn't think I was going to be part of Everton FC by the summer.

7

Finally We Make It

If my moment of truth came in the 1982/3 season, the club's was a year later. On the face of it, we were stronger. Terry Curran had finally made up his mind that he wanted another fling at the First Division and Howard Kendall beat some big competition for Trevor Steven. Everybody had been raving about this whizz-kid from Burnley, especially after a League Cup game at Anfield. What we saw was a skinny little kid, who'd dyed his hair and was so lively in training every day that I thought he must have a key to wind him up. There was no doubting his talent but he suffered a bit like Nev Southall, coming from a small club to a huge one, and it took him a year and an outstanding FA Cup final against Watford before he settled. It didn't help the teenager that we struggled. The back was solid enough, but in midfield and attack we swapped and changed too much and results suffered.

Confidence dipped. We felt the pressure. Players weren't doing in matches what they'd been doing in practice and things went from bad to worse. Crowd aggro against Howard started. When we scrambled past Chesterfield with a draw in the League Cup, we had 8,066 watching that second leg, the lowest crowd in Merseyside history. That was the black night when leaflets were circulated calling for Howard and chairman Philip Carter to get out, saying '30,000 stay-at-home fans can't be wrong, bring back attractive football to Goodison.' That demonstration was the last thing anybody needed. We knew we had the nucleus of a good side. We were still in the Cups and I remembered the previous year when we'd had a bad start and a good finish. All that was needed was the extra confidence to get going. And garbage like that wasn't going to help. The publicity was so bad that Howard briefly banned the press from Bellefield. That was almost the only sign he showed that things were getting to him. He was badly upset when his family were brought into the front line by the graffiti wall writers, but at work he kept as much of the pressure off us as he could. Even though he must have been under terrific strain, there was no change in his approach. He was still laughing and joking and I admired him for that. He never lost his grip, always believing he had an answer in the next game. But I did think he should have been pointing fingers more when things were going wrong instead of taking it all on his back. Colin Harvey would have. He would have given it to us straight if necessary. But Howard never criticized – until we started winning! The fear in the dressing-room was that the board would be panicked into getting rid of him. There was a lot of pressure on them and when chairman Philip Carter gave him his vote of confidence we took it as the kiss of death. But there was never any talk about anyone else coming – and there usually is in those situations – and they stuck with him well. But Howard did himself no favours with the team he put out in the derby at Anfield.

It was the anniversary of the Glenn Keeley farce. Whether his thinking was governed by that I don't know, but he sent us into that game with a five-man midfield and Sharpy alone up front. Adrian Heath was taken out of the firing line and told his job was to look after Sammy Lee. It was a selection that smelled of fear. Every player thought the strategy was wrong;

that we should never worry about another team to that extent. It's my belief that you should let others worry about you. Be positive. I had the feeling from the start of that match that we could not win because there was no way we were going to score. I'd never experienced that before and never since. The biggest indictment of our approach was that for probably the only time in a derby, Liverpool had something you're never allowed – time. They strolled through it, winning 3–0, and to make matters worse our misery was televised. The nation must have wondered if the great passion of Mersey derbies was just a load of hype. Once again, Howard could not admit he was wrong. I was sitting miserably with Sheeds on the coach and we couldn't believe what we heard next. 'If we played them tomorrow,' said the gaffer, 'I'd play the same way again.' We looked at each other and winced. We felt it was completely the wrong way to play.

That was also the day when Peter Reid hit the lowest point of his Everton career – and he wasn't even playing! It seems impossible to believe now, but he was so far out in the cold that he couldn't even make that five-man midfield. It was about that time when Ian St John's radio programme got a phone call on the subject.

'I can't believe Peter Reid's not in the team,' said this lad. 'Be honest, he's the best midfield player they've got. I want to know why he isn't playing week in, week out.'

St John said, 'Thanks very much son. What's your name?'

'Mike.'

'Mike who?'

'Mike Reid.'

'You're no relation, are you?'

'Yeah, I'm his brother!'

When Reidy came in on the Monday, we tried taking the mickey out of him over this but he shrugged and said, 'He's right though, isn't he?' And he was. It was after that he was restored and never left out except for injury. It was after that

I beat 'Sparky' Hughes to the ball in the 1985 FA Cup final.

An early photo with my brother Paul (left) and my sister Helen.

Proud to receive a Deeside Under-11 Schoolboys' trophy. It was just unfortunate that it had to be given out by a Red (Steve Heighway)!

Flint Under-13s. I'm sitting three from the right. On the end of that row to my left is none other than Ian Rush.

Goodison apprentices. In the middle is Steve McMahon (thought to be too lightweight to make the grade) and on the left Paul Lodge who fell foul of Bruce Rioch for his neglectful laundry.

Colin Harvey's 1979 Everton youth team on a tour of France. I'm in the front row, third from the left.

Passions run high in the FA Cup fourth round, January 1981. Here I shout the odds, as Graeme Souness barges referee Clive Thomas.

(*Left*) I always have a determined duel against Rushy, but maybe this is taking things a bit too far.

(*Opposite*) The 1984 FA Cup final. I get in a header in an aerial tussle with Watford's George Reilly.

VECO
ERS

Action from the 1984 Milk Cup final.

After extra time in the goalless first encounter in the Merseyside Milk Cup final.

The sending off of Kevin Moran in the 1985 FA Cup final. Strangely, from that moment on the game went away from us and we ended up losing 1–0 to United's ten men.

Manager and captain embrace at the end of the 1984–85 Championship season.

derby disaster that chairman Carter made the best decision of his life and promoted Colin Harvey to first team coach alongside Mick Heaton.

There's no doubt in my mind about who was the key man of the revival – Colin Harvey. There will be people pointing to Andy Gray, who arrived a few days after Colin's promotion, and to Peter Reid's influence which was to be recognized at last. Both were terrific in what they did. But Colin was the man. I've never met anyone like him. He should have been promoted at the start of that season, or even before. His knowledge and experience were being wasted in the reserves when the first team were struggling. This is saying nothing against Mick Heaton or his ability. They were both good at their jobs. The difference between the two lay in their approach. They are completely different fellas. Mick was called 'Easy' because he was easy-going, someone everyone could get on with. Great for morale. A bubbler. But Colin is a rough type. He snarls at you, winds you up.

In the dressing-room, Mick would give his instructions in a laid back way. Colin will talk to you as if he's actually playing. And if there was a hurtful point to be made, Mick would try to make it in a nice way. Colin? He would give it straight between the eyes. He's one of that breed who will get another ten per cent out of you even if you haven't got it to give. He also had tremendous respect from the lads because he had done it all as a player even if, unbelievably, England only capped him once. That respect was strengthened by the way he drove himself despite the pain in his hips, one of which had to be replaced. He was in a bad way and just looking at this fella forcing himself to run and tackle in the state he was made you realize that you had no excuse for shirking it.

The boss pulled us into the dressing-room to tell us of the change. 'I know the respect you have for Colin. I'm making him first team coach with Mick. Three heads are better than two.' That was the worst moment for both of them. You never saw two professionals looked more embarrassed. There was no mickey-taking. Mick could take as much as you could give, but there's a time and place. He was dejected and hurt. Why not? I would have been in his place. But as time went on he understood and got on with it as a true professional, taking over more of the paperwork and letting Colin get on with much of the training. The kind of spirit Colin Harvey expects from his side showed itself within hours. In the next game, a League Cup tie with Coventry, we were 1–0 down and in trouble when Reidy came on as sub and lifted us. Adrian Heath equalized with twelve minutes left and in the second minute of injury time, Graeme Sharp, who was hobbling with damaged ankle ligaments, threw himself at a cross to win it and send 9,000 of the hard core faithful home with hope.

That game was the turning point for Reidy. He'd felt he was on the way out after the Liverpool game. But he was the sort of player Colin had been and appreciated; a talented, buzzing workhorse, who led by example. Why Howard had taken so long to see what Reidy had to offer was a mystery within the club. When Andy Gray was signed from Wolves, within a week we'd got a trio of winners who hated losing at scrabble let alone soccer. Howard was not keen to get the Scot. Andy was a legend for his bravery. He would head a ball off a bootlace if there was a goal there. But his knee problem wasn't the greatest secret in the game and when the gaffer and Mick went to watch him at Wolves, he showed little and admitted later he was astonished when Everton went through with the deal. The board, who at one point had wanted Howard to go for the Brazilian, Nunes, were under so much strain they had to be seen to be doing something. Howard successfully stalled them over Nunes, who would have been an enormous gamble for a struggling club, and the way things turned out it was lucky he did. Gray's buy was an inspiration, not only for his effect on the club, but the transformation he worked on Sharpy. Andy's another bubbling character you can't shut up.

You could hear him talking in Liverpool when you were in Connah's Quay! And everybody seemed to know him – film stars, pop stars. He was a magnet.

Bad knee or no bad knee, I felt like the fans. We'd signed a player who'd once cost £1 million. We needed a 'name' like that to lift us. And how he did it. He brought new life to the dressing-room. His attitude was powerfully positive and it rubbed off. It was the same on the field. All this from a guy who could be on the treatment table and barely walking one day and the next playing as if nothing's wrong with him. But it's a good job he had players who play to feet. I don't think he could have run after my passes all day! You could do nothing but admire him. The crowd loved him from his first game, a 1–0 win over Forest at Goodison. And from the depths we'd hit against Liverpool just six days before, we were through another round of the League Cup and had won three badly needed points. It was the boost the club desperately needed.

Andy's greatest legacy was the huge difference he made in Sharpy. Graeme and he are chalk and cheese. Aggression wasn't part of Sharpy's game, but was the key to Andy's. It took a helluva lot to wind up this big, strong lad. Gordon Lee had bought Graeme from Dumbarton in a £125,000 deal and it was a big move for a nice, naive young lad. But he was in and out of the side like me and at one point his confidence seemed to go completely. He could have gone back to Scotland. I believe Aberdeen were ready to take him but Howard realized his potential and stuck with him. And Andy completed his education. For a start, Sharpy was bound to be influenced, playing alongside his idol. His eyes were opened at the way Andy battled and threw himself about. They roomed together so Andy had time for plenty of heart-to-hearts. And he taught him a few tricks of the centre-forward's trade, like jumping a little early so he could get his body between the ball and defender. Graeme grew meaner. His touch and confidence improved until he was 100 per cent better. Now he's the best centre-forward in the country, but one who never gets enough credit from outside the game. He certainly didn't when Gary Lineker was banging in the goals for us. But Gary wouldn't have been the same player without Sharpy.

There was to be no miracle transformation in results despite the new blood. Soccer doesn't work like that. There was a lot of grafting to be done. After Forest, we won only one of our next eight League games, scoring three goals. The only bright spot of that period was getting through a tough fourth-round League Cup tie with West Ham after drawing down there. Our Christmas was so bad Santa must have got stuck up the chimney – 0–0 home draws with Sunderland (who'd had Gordon Chisholm sent off) and Coventry, sandwiched a 3–0 disaster at Wolves. That loss at Molineux was the darkest hour before our dawn – one of the worst defeats I've suffered. Wolves, who were later to be relegated, hadn't won at home all season, but everything went wrong for us from the moment David Johnson damaged a hamstring getting up from the dinner table! Then Alan Harper's leg blew up like a balloon and we had to throw in kids Stuart Rimmer and Darren Hughes. What with Nev Southall having a rare off day, the result was a nightmare.

We picked ourselves up at Birmingham in the next game, winning 2–0 on a filthy day, but it was four days later that the FA Cup tie at Stoke really started us going. Our fans have never had enough credit for that. Here we were with a miserable record, clinging on to the Cups as our only hope of taking something from the season and some 10,000 turned out for us as if we were a super team. We couldn't believe or understand the sight of all those blue hordes heading for the Potteries. I suppose they must have thought this might be the last chance we had of doing something and they had better make the most of it. They did. It was just fantastic, and Howard smartly took full advantage. He didn't bother with a team talk. All he did was open the dressing-room window and say, 'Listen to them! You can't let them down. Let's go out and win it for them.' Well, we went out and played as if nothing had been wrong with us all year. You would not have believed it was the same team. That was the moment we took off. From then on, we climbed the League on the backs of the FA Cup and League Cup. Twelve days later, the famous League Cup escape at Oxford only convinced us that fate had finally relented on us. Kevin Brock must be the most famous non-Evertonian in the club's history! Whatever else the midfielder does in the game, he'll be forever remembered around Merseyside as the man whose underhit backpass let in Adrian Heath and let us off the hook in the quarter-final.

Howard had warned us how tough the Third Division club would be. They had already put out Manchester United, Leeds and Newcastle and he reckoned they were particularly dangerous playing down the Manor Ground slope, which was becoming as famous as Yeovil's. We were sceptical. We'd heard all about slopes before and you didn't notice them once you'd started playing. Sure enough on that icy night it wasn't until they were facing up the slope that Bobby McDonald scored, but they were then so full of themselves that I began to think that was it. We were nine minutes away from the exit when Reidy hustled Brock into his mistake and Adrian was on it like a sure-footed ferret, he rounded Steve Hardwick and saved us. To this day, I wonder about fate on that shot. Every time I see the video I expect the ball to drift wide, but somehow it always swings inside the post. In the replay, we turned them over, 4–1, the first time in thirty-one matches that Everton had scored more than twice, and strung passes together like the good team I knew we could be.

At that time, we seemed to be playing Cup ties every other day. It took us three hard games to put out another Third Division side, Gillingham, in the FA Cup fourth round and then it was into the League Cup semi-final with Villa. I'll always remember that first leg at Goodison as Kevin

Richardson's match. The Geordie broke his left wrist, scored the crucial second goal of the 2–0 win and then was terrified we'd mob him. 'Don't touch me! Don't touch me!' he screamed. We just about managed that. But Villa certainly would have liked to have got their hands on him. Right in the last minute, he was on the line for a corner and his arm kept out Gary Shaw's shot. Richo got away with it but the funniest thing was later when he was interviewed on TV. He only agreed to go on if they didn't ask him about the handball, but that was the first question. He tried to bluff his way out of it. When they froze the shot with the ball stuck to his arm, Richo said, 'No, play it on.' And of course when they did that the ball was gone. 'There you are,' he said triumphantly. That save was crucial. I would not like to have gone to Villa Park with just a one-goal lead. We defended well in the return; Derek Mountfield doing a terrific job on Peter Withe, and restricted them to 1–0, a goal scored by Paul Rideout and presented by Andy King's back pass. At the end, I was close to tears. The support we had in that 42,000 crowd was fantastic again, and we just had to go out of the dressing-room and salute them. So, unbelievably, in a season that had promised us nothing but tears, we were at Wembley – and against Liverpool. But for me, the joy and satisfaction of it was less because Mark Higgins would not be alongside me. He had to give in to the pelvic injury that was to kill his Everton career. He hadn't played since we put out West Ham in the fourth round League Cup replay back in December and there was no way he was going to make Wembley. Higgy was destroyed. He'd been all through the bad times and now when the big turnaround was on he could only sit on the sidelines. I felt bad. No disrespect to Derek Mountfield, but I would have loved to have had Higgy alongside. It was as his partner that I made my big break-through and I owed him. We had a great understanding and I've not seen many braver, more full-hearted players. I thought he could have gone on to play for England and there was certainly talk of it. Instead, his career looked in ruins.

I also felt guilty that yet again, through someone's bad luck, I had benefited. I took over the captaincy, not because I was the better man but through Higgy's problem. Not that I want to make any big deal about leading the team out. There are, or should be, eleven captains on the field. The only place you don't find them at our place is when speeches have to be made and suddenly everybody else takes a backward step! But as skipper you do have a terrific bonus – the chance to get your hands on a cup first. There's no better feeling than doing that at Wembley and I'd have loved Higgy to have experienced that. Getting to the old stadium was as much his triumph as mine and I tried to make him feel part of the squad as much as I could. When we won the FA Cup, I made sure he carried it after the celebrations.

There were many people who believed Everton's name was already on the League Cup after our great escape at Oxford, but our luck ran out in the final. The way the match went, you wouldn't have thought there was any difference between us and Liverpool. At times, we knocked the ball about as if they were the underdogs. We should have won it in the first half-hour when we had them reeling. But we were twice let down by Fareham referee Alan Robinson, a man whose name figures large in Everton history for the wrong reasons. He did nothing at the crucial moment when Phil Neal clipped Kevin Sheedy's heels – the start of Sheeds' ankle problems – when he was through. And, even more blatantly, he failed to react after Adrian Heath shot past Bruce Grobbelaar and Alan Hansen carried the ball along the goal line, almost as if he was leading the team out again. How, I don't know. If the referee was unsighted, his linesman seemed to have a clear view. Maybe neither could believe what they were seeing! Whatever, you have to learn to live with these things in football. Look at Maradona's handball in Mexico. Maybe the Hansen episode was someone evening up the score after Kevin Richardson's semi-final 'save'! Anyway, we should have wrapped it up without that. You don't give Liverpool second chances. We did and paid for it.

Three days later, we were beaten 1–0 in the replay at Maine Road and they just about earned it even if Graeme Souness' goal was a freak on two counts. First, Suey managed to turn me and, good as he is, he'd never done that to me in his life. It happened because, ironically, his touch let him down for once. His control is usually so good, but this time he mis-controlled the ball and as a result I mis-read it. Second, he fired in from outside the box and I couldn't believe anyone could beat Neville from that range. There were a few tears that night – and almost a lot of pain. As we went back through Manchester's Moss Side in the coach, I saw a lad draw back his arm. I shouted 'brick' and slid down in my seat. It was a brick and it smashed through the window behind me, luckily hitting nobody. It was a sour finish to a sour evening. But, overall, there was some consolation. At Wembley our fans had played a full part with Liverpool's in making what the Metropolitan police called 'the friendly final.' It was the same at Maine Road. I doubt if any other city could send its major clubs to battle together and be able to boast of fans' behaviour like that.

Wc were shattered at losing out to Liverpool but not flattened. It was a case of 'One final's gone, let's get on with the next.' Our fans, out in force for the FA Cup semi-final with Southampton, summed up our feelings perfectly at Highbury when they sang, 'Tell me Ma to put the champagne on ice, we're going to Wembley twice.' With Watford and Plymouth in the other semi we knew we'd never have a better chance. Like most semi-finals, it was close and hard against Southampton, but the only one of us in real trouble that day was me. Reidy and me both have big behinds and for some reason there was only one pair of shorts big enough to suit us. He got to them first and I went out and suffered through forty-five minutes in a pair that Twiggy might have found tight. I felt bad and played the same way. When I got in at half-time, Reidy said, 'What's the matter with you? You were awful.' I told him and without hesitating he took those shorts off, hurled them at me and said, 'Right, you've got them.' I accepted gratefully and from then on felt as if I'd been released.

Nev needed to make a few saves which, with Peter Shilton not having one of his best days, prompted Howard to say his man was now Britain's best. What with Nev's brilliance and our missing chances, at ninety minutes it was still 0–0. It was then that Frank Worthington came up and wanted to shake hands. He thought it was the end. I put him off, saying, 'Sorry, Frank. It's extra time.' He groaned and said, 'Oh no it's not, is it?' They were the words of a man whose legs had gone. I felt then we would win. Howard had said his fitness wasn't too clever and at every set piece we worked on weakening it some more, sending Derek Mountfield forward. It was Derek who caused the only goal after 117 minutes. He flicked on Reidy's free kick and Adrian Heath timed his header brilliantly from an awkwardly bouncing ball.

We were at Wembley again. And in the final against Watford. I've never seen one team as heavily supported as we were. There was blue and white everywhere. But, if there weren't so many of them, Watford's fans made up for it in quality, shaking hands and being friendly with everyone. They're a real family club and it showed. There was no trouble and the family could actually relax and concentrate on the day. And that was just about what the gaffer's orders were about. 'You're going to enjoy the day,' he said, 'no matter what happens. Just make sure you go out and play.' He wasn't too concerned about Watford. We were just told to beware of John Barnes' tricks, their early ball stuff and long throw-ins. We did everything that was asked of us, helped by the experience of having been at Wembley. Watford were a young side. Their back four – David Bardsley (nineteen), Steve Terry (twenty-one), Lee Sinnott (eighteen), Paul Price (twenty) – was the youngest defensive line-up in Cup Final history. And our kid, Trevor Steven, took full advantage. Maybe we wanted to win a little more than they did. Some of us, including me, thought it might be our last chance. We worked on the two young full-backs and Trevor was so good, Price was taken off and Kenny Jackett stuck back there to look after him.

It was Trevor who set us on the way after thirty-eight minutes. His drive hit Sharpy who killed the ball and fired past Steve Sherwood. That settled us down and we never looked back. Seven minutes after half-time came the most discussed part of the final, the goal by Andy Gray which finished them off. Steven slung over a juicy cross which Andy was almost licking his lips over. Sherwood reached the ball but lost it in the challenge and Andy claimed it. It was a good old-fashioned centre-forward's goal which referees too often disallow and Leicester's John Hunting did well. If anybody deserved that break it was Andy. He'd been a key figure in putting fight back into the club. Every game was like World War II to him and he earned that reward. The second half was the quickest forty-five minutes I've known. I couldn't believe it when I asked the ref how long was left and he said, 'Two minutes.' The only worry I'd had after Andy's goal was whether I'd be able to lift the Cup at the end. I had fallen on my shoulder before half-time in a challenge with big George Reilly. Despite ice and heat treatment at the break, by the end I could hardly lift the arm it was so sore. But when it came to the moment I could probably have lifted the Titanic, no trouble. That first trophy was especially sweet for Howard Kendall. He learned and we learned a lot from that strange season. Mainly it came down to knowing who your friends were when things were going badly. Who believed in you and who didn't. And those people who'd been so quick to get the boot in during the bad times would suffer in the success years.

8

Now for the Big One

The lads left for a week's break in Magaluf believing that the FA Cup triumph was only the start and that next season we would be pushing for the big one – the championship that had not been Everton's since 1970. When we achieved it, throwing in the Cup Winner's Cup and nearly the FA Cup as well, we had rid the club of a fifteen-year torment. Every side since Catterick's had been measured painfully against his. It was forever rammed down our throats. They had set the modern standard and the legend of that line-up grew and was probably exaggerated with every telling of the story. I understood it. It was that side that had made me fall in love with the place. It was special. But when the club struggled after Catterick, the memory became an embarrassment. Colin Harvey, the last survivor of that side at the club until Howard Kendall returned, hated talking about it publicly. He feared it was only twisting the knife in a deepening wound.

Just to add to the problem of Catterick's successors, it wasn't enough for Everton to win. They had to do it in a way that followed the old 'school of science' tradition. I believe we stayed faithful to that tradition and now all those backward looks at the good old days are being replaced by people looking forward to the time when we break Liverpool's record. The talk is of us, not of the past. Maybe Steven–Reid–Bracewell–Sheedy doesn't have the same ring to it as Harvey–Kendall–Ball, but that midfield will be just as revered in future Everton histories, and so it should be. Two buzzers in the middle feeding the most direct right-winger since Steve Coppell and the best left foot I know. The balance was perfect and the effect usually irresistible. Yet, when Paul Bracewell was brought in from Sunderland just after we had beaten Watford in the Cup Final, I didn't see why we needed him. I thought Kevin Richardson would have done well alongside Reidy. Here was a good player with a good touch and strength. And he could score goals. There was also a fear that Brace and Reidy would be too alike in style. But Howard Kendall was spot on. Brace and Reidy mixed so well together. Their understanding was terrific and they would rarely be more than ten yards apart. If someone got through Reidy's tackle there would be Brace, waiting. I don't think Brace had enough credit for what he did that year. It's his fate to be one of those players who's more appreciated on the field than off it. He hasn't a great amount of speed but what he has he uses for ninety minutes. He puts people under such pressure that he forces them into mistakes. I'm told he was an awful passer at Stoke, but he is the reverse with us. Maybe it was the fact that he had the confidence of knowing people were confident in him.

Brace wasn't the only new recruit. It was also the time Howard Kendall took a gamble on Pat Van den Hauwe. The left-back with the killer look and 'Psycho-Pat' nickname had his hell-raising moments with Birmingham and there were a few managers who wouldn't have touched him. But Jim Smith had managed him at Birmingham and his recommendation was good enough for Howard. The gamble certainly paid off. Pat gave us extra steel and pace. As for off the field, the lads emphasized to him that stepping out of line at Everton isn't the same as at Birmingham. It's all the way round the city before you know where you are and Everton's reputation isn't something to be messed with. I think he got the message. The only time that he really got into trouble was when we couldn't blame him because most of us were involved, too. That was at QPR, not long after he came, when he and Simon Stainrod were sent off after a bust-up. There were about eighteen players having a right old ding-dong in the middle of the plastic. It wasn't pretty, but if there's any trouble, we like to get round and support. Our only two not involved were Sheeds and Nev. It wasn't Sheeds' habit to get mixed up in things like that and nothing seems to worry Nev. After that, the standing joke was 'remember that time at QPR when Sheeds was ten yards away directing the battle. Just like Montgomery.'

Our confidence for the big title push wasn't done any harm when we got some revenge against Liverpool in the Charity Shield at Wembley. But it was when we next met that we achieved what was one of the key results – maybe THE key one – of our advance. We had taken a while to hit our stride, losing the first two games of the season, starting 1–4 at home to Spurs. Our duck was broken in a televised game at Chelsea where we went out determined to show we were no one-season wonders. We had scares in the Cup Winners' Cup against Ireland's UCD and Sheffield United in the League Cup, but we were starting to motor by the time we went to Anfield on 20th October. I felt it was time we made a point there if we were going to show we were ready to match them. Everton hadn't known what it was like to win there in fourteen years. It was also the place where the pain of the previous year's self-inflicted wound was still strong. This time we did everything we'd hoped to do. It was one of the best games we'd played there. They never troubled us in the first half and created nothing in the second. Meanwhile, Sharpy won it for us with a goal that will stay part of the Mersey legend, a thirty-yard volley two minutes after half-time; and there could have been more.

It was the psychological breakthrough. If we could win there, who had we to fear? Buoyed up, we won in Bratislava to keep our European hopes bubbling and the next League game sent Grandpa Ratcliffe into mourning by crushing his beloved Manchester United, 5–0. It was a performance which Howard Kendall said was 'the best I've known as a manager anywhere.' We were top by November and that's where we stayed except for a three-week spell when we stuttered around Christmas. During that period, there were only two real setbacks. Grimsby put us out of the League Cup, 1–0, at Goodison where we had nineteen corners. But Howard turned even that to our advantage by buying the scorer of the last-minute goal, Paul Wilkinson. And Adrian Heath, who had stormed through the opening three months with eleven League goals in seventeen games, had his knee ligaments wrecked in a challenge with Sheffield Wednesday's Brian Marwood and was out for the season. But with Andy Gray champing at the bit, we even rode that loss.

The other key result of the campaign came at Sunderland on Boxing Day. We'd gone through a spell of winning one out of five games, including an unbelievable 3–4 home defeat by Chelsea in which Gordon Davies, who was only playing because David Speedie was injured, hit the perfect hat-trick –left foot, right foot and head. We needed to do something at Roker Park. People had started questioning us, wondering whether the bubble had burst. There were also Jeremiahs who kept saying Everton faded over Christmas. Roker wasn't a good ground for me. I'd never had any joy there – but Andy Gray had never lost there. Mind you, I'm not sure he had any bogey grounds. He wasn't the type to admit things like that. We also had Paul Bracewell wanting to make a personal point. He had a little chip on his shoulder about the manager, Len Ashurst, and some of the other players after his experiences there. With him in that mood, it didn't do our cause any harm, and we were great that day, winning 2–1 with goals by Derek Mountfield.

That set us off. Including that win, we won sixteen and drew two of the next eighteen League games, conceding nine goals. I doubt if that run has been matched, especially at that vital stage. Not even Liverpool could live with that. It got to the stage when we went out never thinking we could lose – and that's a rare feeling to savour. It was also a feeling that was never tested harder than in the sixth round and semi-final of the FA Cup. First, Ipswich gave us a tremendous fright at Goodison. I thought we were dead and gone when Derek Mountfield showed again his knack of being in the right place at the right time, striking late to give us another chance at 2–2. We just about deserved to scrape through over there, Sharpy shooting in a penalty for a foul on himself. But the decision was the kind you don't expect to get as an away team. We'd gone out with the attitude that it must be our year again. And the 'semi' with Luton at Villa Park only seemed to prove it.

We went into that game with legs deadened after the huge effort put into the first leg of the Cup Winners' Cup semi-final with Bayern Munich in Germany in midweek. We hadn't started playing when Ricky Hill scored after thirty-seven minutes. It followed an unseen foul by Brian Stein on Gary Stevens but Luton had earned it. We were just five minutes from giving up the Cup when Kevin Sheedy equalized with a free kick that I didn't think we should have had. It wasn't one of his specials. It must have bounced five times on the way in but we wouldn't have been bothered if it had gone in off his nose by then. I was down on my knees on the half-way line. Up in the stand, Debbie Sheedy must have been torn between joy and blowing raspberries at the bigmouths who had been giving her earache over her Kevin. The truth was that Howard had taken a gamble on Sheeds, who was troubled by an ankle and wasn't really fit. But all the fans saw was an ex-Liverpudlian struggling to put a pass right. All through the match he was getting stick and Sharon said she felt sorry for Debbie who could not help but hear the swearing and abuse directed at her man.

When he scored, I was so pleased for the fellow. Of course, the fans mobbed him and I wouldn't have blamed him if he'd told them where to go. Not surprisingly, that equalizer, coming when they could just about see Wembley's twin towers, knocked the heart out of Luton. After that there was only going to be one winner. Five minutes away from a replay, it was Sheeds again, throwing in another free kick and Derek Mountfield headed us back to Wembley. At that time, we were in the middle of a ten-game winning streak in the League, but we didn't wrap up the title until the start of May. Then in three glorious days, we became only the second team to win at Sheffield Wednesday that season – a victory which included a save by Neville off Imre Varadi that was special even for him – and beat QPR at home, 2–0, before a 50,000 crowd. The only pity was the League seemed to be caught with their pants down. Or maybe they were used to going to Anfield! Whatever the reason, we had to wait another two days to get our hands on that trophy from League president Jack Dunnett before the home win over West Ham. But it was still very sweet.

9

Final Fear

Nobody would argue that Bayern Munich gave us our biggest test in the Cup Winners' Cup. I've never played in such a game as the second leg of that semi-final at Goodison in April 1985. It will be talked about on Merseyside as long as that Liverpool–St Etienne European Cup nail-biter of a few years back. But it wasn't the hard, skilled Germans who gave us our biggest scare in Europe. The team that did that was probably the least regarded in the competition – the part-timers of Dublin's University College. That's a team we would probably beat 999 times out of a thousand. But this wasn't a matter of form or quality. Nor was it what they did, wholehearted though they were. It wouldn't have mattered who we faced in that first round. It was the first European club game for all of us and we dreaded making a mess of it. Everton's record in Europe had not been good. Even the great 1970 side survived only two rounds of the European Cup. As a raw eighteen-year-old, I was a sub for the home leg when Everton's last adventure on the continent had ended at the first try, 2–0, against Feyenoord in the 1979/80 UEFA Cup. Everton were 1–0 down from the first leg and George Wood was harshly blamed when the Dutch repeated the scoreline at Goodison. True, the ball went under the keeper's arm, but I happened to be right behind him at that moment and the ball must have swerved four or five times in the air.

I remembered the disappointment of that night and didn't fancy it again. Anyway, we got a 0–0 result in Dublin, which on the face of it, seemed to give us a platform to break loose at home. It didn't happen, although Sharpy scored after ten minutes. If we were edgy over there, it was worse at Goodison. I was really uptight and Reidy even worse. We were terrified of being caught on the break and conceding an away goal. They had Joe Hanrahan up front, a lad everyone was talking about at the time and who eventually went to Manchester United. He did look good which made us even more watchful. UCD were also hard to break down and the final whistle couldn't come quick enough for us or the crowd. We were a different team with that first hurdle out of the way.

The worst the Czechs of Inter Bratislava could do was make us walk the longest players' tunnel – it must have been a mile – that I've known. We gave them credit for being a better team than they were and played accordingly. Paul Bracewell scored with a rare header early on and we were never stretched while holding that lead. The return was a 3–0 stroll.

Fortuna Sittard were a better team in the third round but even less of a problem because we played so well. The Dutch were utterly unable to handle the pressure we put on them, or Andy Gray, a centre-forward of a type they had probably never met and thought hadn't existed since Bobby Smith packed up. Andy killed them off at Goodison with a typically brave hat-trick. And when Sharpy scored early over there, the only interest left was whether the fellow who ran on the pitch naked would leave with everything intact. He got stuck trying to climb the pitch fence and police dogs were eyeing him as if they fancied a meat and two veg dinner!

Then came Bayern – and a different ball game. We had to take them on over there, plus a 70,000 crowd, without the injured Andy and Sheeds. Trevor Steven went up front with Sharpy and for the first twenty-five minutes we were under a lot of pressure. Nev had some adventures and Kevin Richardson kicked off the line from Michael Rummenigge. Not until the second half did we get enough of the ball to put them under any kind of pressure and then Sharpy had probably the best chance of the game. We finished 0–0 and looked to have one foot in the final, but we knew there was plenty to do. We had nearly 50,000 at Goodison for the return and with the red-hot atmosphere created by the massed Evertonians we could have run through hell and not noticed. Those fans probably sucked in a couple of goals. They were so wound up that when Terry Darracott tried to stop coins being thrown at the German bench, they even turned on him, spitting and chucking more coins. That cost the club a £2,000 fine. The tension of the night showed when someone as experienced as Andy Gray got himself involved in a feud with Pflugler who kicked him and paid for it. Then Eder collapsed with a broken nose, cut from nose to lip, when Andy's back header missed the ball but not him.

Reidy, as usual, was an advert for our spirit that night. He and the Dane, Soren Lerby, had a duel which involved some juicy tackles. One cut Peter's leg badly enough to need the physiotherapist, John Clinkard. 'You'll need stitches in that,' said Clinks. But Reidy knew the German bench were watching closely and didn't want to show any sign of weakness. He picked up a sponge, jammed it inside his blooded sock, saying, 'this'll do', and went back to the battle as if nothing had changed. Not until after the game did he have that leg stitched. It was at that point that manager Uli Hoeness stalked from his bench, hands deep inside his Gestapo-like raincoat, and said to Howard, 'This is not football, Mr Kendall.' As one man, the bench told him in two words he was out of order!

We put them under a lot of pressure, but they would not buckle easily and gave us problems. Kogl, their quick, clever left-winger, who had a brilliant first half, laid on a goal for Hoeness after thirty-eight minutes and 50,000 people have never been quieter. Even after that blow, we never stopped believing we would win. The orders at half-time were short and simple – forget the fancy bits and just bomb their penalty area. And that's what got us the result. Within three minutes, Sharpy had kept up his record of scoring in every round. The Germans became more and more frightened of our tartan terrors. It was Andy who shot us ahead and, with Bayern desperately going for an away goal, Trevor Steven put the tie out of their reach. Their coach Udo Lattek said, 'On this showing, Everton are the best in Europe.' You might not have got an argument about that at Anfield just then.

It was right that we should meet a team named Rapid in the Cup Winners Cup final. That just about summed up our approach and finish to that fantastic May night in Rotterdam. Games had been coming so thick and fast while we headed for the treble, we just didn't have time to think too long about the importance of them or get nervous. That's one of the reasons why we got so far that year. Meeting the Viennese was just another job to be done. At least we felt that way until we walked out of the tunnel in Feyenoord's fine stadium. There was a sight I'll never forget – 20,000, maybe more, Evertonians jampacked into their section, willing us to put our first European pot on the sideboard. They'd had to suffer for years while various European silver had ended up at Anfield. Now they could sense we were about to start our own collection. I've never seen as many of our fans travel that far. It put a lump in my throat and I felt that if we couldn't do it for them, we couldn't do it for anyone.

Apart from our fans, there were nearly a thousand Celtic supporters backing us. We often get them at Goodison if Celtic have no game, but this was special to them. Rapid had been beaten by their team in the second round but got a reprieve. They were given a replay at Old Trafford because a bottle had been thrown in the second leg at Parkhead. The fans wanted us to do a revenge job and we were happy to oblige. Bayern had been our final as a test of technique and guts, but Rapid looked no mugs on paper. Their win over Celtic was controversial but they had also put out Dynamo Moscow 4–2 on aggregate in the semi-final, and Dynamo Dresden, 5–3, in the quarters. We knew Hans Krankl, the Austrian international striker, had a terrific shot and could be dangerous although he was over the hill. And I was happy Antonin Panenka, the Czech midfielder, was only a sub. I'd played against him for Wales and reckoned he was a great player.

Well, we just went out and played our normal game and did it well. I think we earned increased respect among a lot of people that night. It got Everton on the big map again. Not because of the result so much but because of the way we achieved it. We were made the European Team of the Year, and played like it. There were only two periods of worry – when we were still 0–0 at half-time despite dominating, and when Krankl dragged us back to 2–1. It's not good to dominate the first half of a match and get nothing for it. The other side can grow in confidence and strength when they have survived a grilling like that. But Howard Kendall didn't panic. He said what he always says in those situations, 'Keep it going and the goals will come. Don't worry and don't try anything different.'

Sure enough, Andy Gray put away a volley twelve minutes later and Trevor Steven struck the second at the back stick from Sheeds' corner. At that point, maybe mistakenly, we tried to slow the game down and eased off the pressure. They stuck Panenka on and Rapid came alive. A firecracker which exploded on the pitch didn't do my insides any good but that was not to be our only frightener. Krankl scored with a shot through my legs and suddenly it was a game again. We had to raise our game and pace, fast. Luckily enough, Sheeds struck a brilliant twenty-five yarder two minutes later and killed them off. That goal illustrated one of the best things about our team – the way we felt we could always go up a gear and grab a goal when it was needed. That happened so many times.

Krankl was generous, saying, 'Everton were just too good. It's been a long time since we played against anyone of their class. They are possibly the best side in Europe.' He'd have an argument about the 'possibly'! All the family were there although brother Paul, or 'Charlie' as we know him, was taking in the atmosphere on the terraces. He's such a fanatic I had to find him and take the Cup over. When I got to the fence, there he was, tears in his eyes. And alongside him was our priest, Father Crane, jumping up and down on the railings. Unforgettable. My dad was choked as well. But we didn't have long to savour all the glory. United and the Cup Final were only days away and we flew straight back that night. We had a few drinks on the plane and that was the celebration. We had Thursday off and then it was down to our Cup Final hotel near Watford. We were buzzing and we wanted that treble to round it off.

I never thought I'd see the day when I'd be relieved to lose a Cup Final – but I was when Manchester United beat us. It could have been the greatest day of our lives – the climax to an incredible year. We were going for a unique treble after taking the League and, three days before, the Cup Winners' Cup. Well before the end, the possibility of re-writing record books had become secondary. I have never been so frightened or disturbed on a football pitch as I was that May day. Looking back, Heysel was still eleven days away, but I believe there was danger of something worse happening at Wembley or outside it, the atmosphere was so terrible. The cause was one mistaken act – Kevin Moran's sending off by referee Peter Willis in the second half.

Moran had sent Peter Reid crashing as he looked like breaking clear. But the decision was wrong and I told Willis so. Sure he caught him, but I saw nothing malicious in the tackle.

It was a ball he had to go for and was probably favourite to get. It looked bad because Reidy had just got a little touch before Moran lunged in, nicking the ball away and leaving the Irishman to catch him low. I accept the ref took into account that Kevin was the last man in defence and that if he had been beaten Reidy was away. But I've seen that tackle on video again and again and if it had been me in Kevin's position I would have gone for that ball.

I've never felt so sorry for anyone in my life as I was for him. To get sent off at Wembley is a terrible punishment. I even asked the ref not to take that step and it's not like me to do that. 'You've got to be joking,' I said. 'You can't send him off for that.' Reidy, who wasn't injured by the tackle, also pleaded. But, no good, he had to go. Kevin couldn't believe it. He looked utterly shocked and I couldn't blame him. He's hard and enthusiastic but not dirty. It would have been fair enough if he'd kicked somebody deliberately or thrown a punch. But not for that. And then not to allow him to collect his medal on the pitch was a disgrace.

That incident changed the game, lifting the ten men as it so often does. Until then, they'd not made a chance. But it was what it did to the crowd that worried me. There were a lot more United fans there than Everton and they were boiling mad. The atmosphere between Manchester and Merseyside supporters has not been good for some time and there it was poisonous. Some of the chants that were coming up were really bad and ugly. I was scared the whole thing was going to erupt and that if we won there would be real trouble. I'd never felt like that in a match and I always thought it was something that would never bother me. But it did, badly. It wasn't my safety I was concerned about, but Sharon's and the family's. Mum and Dad, Nan and Grandad, aunts and uncles were all in the stand and I feared what might happen to them, particularly when they got outside the stadium and made the long walk to the coach.

We put United under pressure after Moran had gone but didn't do much with it, and by that time I was in two minds about what I wanted the result to be. Then in extra time, Norman Whiteside prevented what could have been a load of trouble with what at the time looked like a great goal. I changed my mind after seeing the playback. Neville Southall is not one of those keepers who blames everyone but himself for a goal and when he saw that video he held up his hands. Norman, far out on the right, put a heck of a curl on the ball which finished just inside the far post. But the film shows Nev was only an inch away from it and he had started from a bad position, almost stuck to the post when he dived. But you can't knock him for that when you think how many times he's saved us. He's worth a few points a year, the difference between winning and losing honours. We never looked like scoring after that goal. They defended well but we played into their hands, never getting people wide to get in crosses. But, at the end, the sadness that we had lost was second to 'thank God, Sharon and the family will be all right now.'

It's odd now to think, looking back, that we were too relaxed going into that final. I said before the European win in Rotterdam that we were helped by being relaxed, but that can be overdone. We could have done with a bit more edginess and nervousness. It's always difficult to play a British team after a foreign one because the styles are so completely different. But that wasn't really the problem here. We were just too confident that we were going to make history. Also, our attitude was probably coloured by the fact that we'd had the better of United over the years and they had a bit of a complex about us. There was another possible factor in our performance – battle fatigue. We'd played more games than anybody else. If I hadn't missed the last League game with Luton after tweaking a knee in the garden while playing with the kids, I'd have played sixty-eight games that season, including internationals, which would have been a record for any player other than a keeper.

But, overall, it was an occasion, like Heysel, when I felt that Bill Shankly's crack about soccer being more important than life or death was way off the mark.

10

Heysel Horror

I had a little taster of the agony suffered by the bereaved after the horror of Heysel. My cousin, John, was supposed to go to that Liverpool–Juventus European Cup final. And it wasn't until a day later that we found out that he hadn't gone to Brussels. My Aunty Jo had been worried to death, and who could blame her? I felt for Rushy and all the lads across the park who had family and friends over there and were wondering what was happening to them while they were trying to get their minds on the match. I know I couldn't believe my eyes and I was only watching on TV. I had got back late for the match and thought I'd missed the first half-hour. Then when I switched on and found people not talking about football but about how many were dead I just couldn't take it in.

When the first reaction of shock and horror had gone it was then that the talk came about the English facing a ban and suddenly I realized, selfishly I know, exactly what it would mean to Everton and me. Just two weeks previously we had won the Cup Winners Cup against Rapid Vienna and there had not been a scrap of trouble in Rotterdam. Now, through absolutely no fault of ours or our fans, we were to be deprived of going for the biggest club prize of the lot at a time when there was plenty to suggest we were the best in Europe. It was something we had worked hard for and we were on a high. The poor quality of the Barcelona–Steaua final the next year only made us feel worse. There is a deep sense of shame among Liverpool fans over what happened. They did the damage but they shouldn't carry the can. The Belgians took a ridiculous risk selling tickets to both sets of supporters at one end, and UEFA chose a ground where facilities for safety weren't good enough. In future, football's European chiefs must allow themselves the chance to think again about a venue when finalists are teams with massive supports like Liverpool and Juventus. They should choose somewhere those fans are going to be as sure as they can be that they won't lose blood, let alone lives. Feyenoord got it exactly right for our game with Rapid. There were great gaps in the support at the Austrian end of the ground because they had refused to sell tickets to casual buyers and their segregation was good. It's terrible that such a thing should be necessary to watch a football match, but it is, and I don't understand why the Belgians weren't better prepared, especially knowing they have thousands of Italian expatriates living in Brussels.

People still don't realize how organized terrace violence is. It's a kind of Mafia situation, with soldiers and colonels, and the people who organize the trouble often get away with it. It's the kids of sixteen to nineteen who get caught while the older ones disappear when the trouble starts. It was a terrible blow for us to be out of Europe and there was a fear that it might flatten people at the club. But when we'd got over the first disappointment about what the ban meant for us, we knew if a stand wasn't taken, hooliganism could kill the game. Something had to be done and whatever we might think about the justice of punishing clubs for their supporters' madness it did seem to stop the rot for a while. What disappointed me when the mess was cleared up was the lack of speed with which justice was meted out. Whatever the rights and wrongs of twenty-six getting the blame for thirty-nine people's deaths, once they had been rounded up they should have been sent back to Belgium quicker. That would have given Europe some faith that we were trying to put our house in order as quickly as possible. Had that been done it might have speeded up our re-entry into Europe.

Merseyside needed a lift after the Heysel disaster and it seemed a good idea when someone from the Prudential insurance company asked Everton and Liverpool to get together for a joint team photograph. The plan was to emphasize what the two clubs do anyway – show that even such fierce rivals can unite and forget once the battle is over. The picture was to be distributed to schools under the title 'Mersey unites' and players from each club were to provide back-up with visits. But the organizers hadn't allowed for the fact that our rivalry is real and includes not liking to be photographed on the other's territory. It might sound petty to outsiders, especially when considering the tragedy that sparked the idea, but by the time this picture project came up, past events had hardened our attitude. It had become a matter of principle to us and we weren't going to budge.

What was sticking in our throats was that every time we had done something of the kind with Liverpool – and it's been a few times – it seemed to end up with us going there, never them coming to us. We were just a little sick of it. So this time we thought, 'Right, they're coming to our place for this, no matter what.' They dug their heels in, stalled and hedged. So did we. The result was that it was six months before the idea became fact. I know it's nothing to be proud of and maybe we made our stand at the wrong time, but that's the way we felt. The saga was only ended when Howard rang Kenny and said, 'Look, you pass Bellefield every day on your way to training. Why not pop in one morning and let's get it done.' And that's what happened. Even then they arrived late. We were changed and ready by the time they arrived. And the affair wasn't over yet.

It was a bitter, cold, November day and neither team wanted to be first out of the dressing-room and into that wind. I went upstairs for a cup of tea. I gather it was Peter Reid who broke the deadlock, grabbing Kenny and saying, 'For crying out loud, let's get out there and get it done.' And that's how it was. Then we found the men from the Pru weren't in it just for being nice to fellow humans. Business came into it. They tried to cash in on the pictures, especially when we reached the FA Cup final. Eventually, we were given some compensation through agent Eric Hall. But Kenny wasn't satisfied with what was offered. He took over negotiations and got us more. So it worked out well for us in the end, but I believe it worked out even better for those crafty so and so's from the Pru.

11

Links, United and Brace

Howard Kendall showed the strength and instinct of a true manager when he let Andy Gray go and bought Gary Lineker. Evertonians were outraged over Andy leaving. They couldn't believe that one of the great heroes of the turnaround had been allowed to go almost before the joy of the 1985 championship had died. The letters of protest could have covered Howard's wall. The lads would have liked Andy to stay because of his character and humour, let alone his playing qualities, and I could not understand why Graham Taylor did not keep him at Villa when he took over. Even if he could only crawl into the dressing-room, Andy's just the man you want when the going gets tough. He'll make a great coach – maybe another Colin Harvey. But everybody at Goodison realized he didn't have many games left in him.

If we played fifty-five games, you could expect him to be in about thirty because of his knees. We called him 'the Iceman' because every Monday morning he'd either be on ice or he'd be taking it home. Howard realized he wouldn't get his money back in six or even fewer months and when Villa made him a great offer, he couldn't refuse it. He obviously had Lineker in mind when that deal went through. To be honest – and I know it sounds daft now – I didn't know whether Gary would be up to it. Despite his goals at Leicester, he had never shown me that he was an Everton player. He'd never caused us much problem and struck me as a little lazy; but if anything was going to change him it was our lads and the manager. Sure enough, he had a great year, even though he had to survive a difficult few months. We knew we had to adapt to him to get the best out of his tremendous speed. That meant sacrificing a little time in our build-up and playing the ball quicker than we were used to.

Many fans weren't happy about that. They couldn't see anything wrong with the style that had won us two trophies the year before and they weren't slow to tell us. There was also the fact that they were still shouting for their favourite, Andy, even though Gary was scoring consistently. You could only guess what stick he'd have taken if he hadn't been scoring. And that did concern even the unflappable Links, although he hid it well. It also worried the lads. If that wasn't enough, he was also doing his stuff despite only being able to train on two days a week. He spent a lot of his time in the treatment room because of a little pelvic strain and we gave him a lot of chat over that.

He only used to come out training Thursday and Friday. Sometimes only Friday. He didn't need injections, just rest. And that was where the gaffer was great. As long as you did it for him on the Saturday, you could have as much time off as you wanted if the reasons were right. They were right for Links because that strain did trouble him. When he did train, he was never at his sharpest. He kept himself for the matches – and how that paid off. He just seemed to explode into action. He was lightning. It took until just after Boxing Day before he really won the fans over. It was then that he scored two vital goals in a hard match against Sheffield Wednesday and got an ovation. He was in. He'd ridden all that extra pressure really well, and went on to change completely as a player over the year. I reckon he improved 100 per cent.

When he first arrived, he couldn't go past players unless the ball was played over the top for him to use that burning pace. But, by the end, he was holding it up and then going past players, which was something I didn't think he could do. It's amazing the confidence you get when you're scoring a few goals. I had a great understanding with him. I knew exactly when he was ready to go on one of his runs and even if my pass wasn't good, he could make it good with that speed. But a lot of his success was down to Sharpy and the way he cleverly adapted to him. Their partnership suited Gary down to the ground, and how we profited. Sharpy would take a load of weight off him. He was great at holding the ball up and then giving Gary the little flick-ons which he thrived on.

That's why we were great on the break and it was inevitable that there would be time when we missed his speed. He was also so sharp in the box. He'd reach things with his boot others could reach only with their heads. He also got many goals with his head and that was something he wasn't noted for. To think he scored forty goals that season and we won nothing. What that did was explode the myth that to win the title you need a twenty-goal man. In our two championship years the goals were spread around.

Gary never told the lads he was leaving for Barcelona, and I could understand it. The lads would have been taking the mickey for ever. Nobody blamed him for taking the money. It gave him security and nobody in this precarious profession would begrudge him that.

Gary Lineker's incredible campaign coincided with the year that Manchester United's unofficial publicity men, the media, brainwashed the public into believing that the championship lasted fifteen games. That's how long they went unbeaten and suddenly they were being hailed not only as kings but also as the first team that could walk on water. The fact that there was three-quarters of the season left didn't seem to matter. Everton were never out of the top ten, despite our injuries, while they

(*Above*) Putting in a solid challenge on Craig Johnston at Goodison Park.

(*Right*) More action from a Merseyside derby.

With Neville Southall and Pat Van den Hauwe – the other Welsh internationals at Everton.

Mike England directing operations at a Welsh training session. He was always popular with the players, who were sorry to see him sacked by the Welsh FA.

The Evertonians on the bench celebrate our semi-final victory over Southampton at Highbury in 1986. Colin's tremendous commitment to the game is perfectly captured by his expression.

My brother Paul, Adrian 'Inchy' Heath and my friend Jakey (from left to right) at an after-match dinner.

Andy Gray with a typically courageous diving header puts us on our way to victory in the European Cup-Winners' Cup against Fortuna Sittard in the quarter-finals (March 1985).

Elation as I lift the European Cup-Winners' Cup for the Blues.

I go over to the Everton fans and show the trophy to my brother.

The 1986 European Cup-Winners' Cup winners. None of the lads knows who the guy on the extreme left is, but he got his face in all the team photos that night.

Hawaiian holiday, with Terry Darracott and Howard Kendall.

It's not too often that I get my name on the score-sheet, and it's all the sweeter when it's against Liverpool.

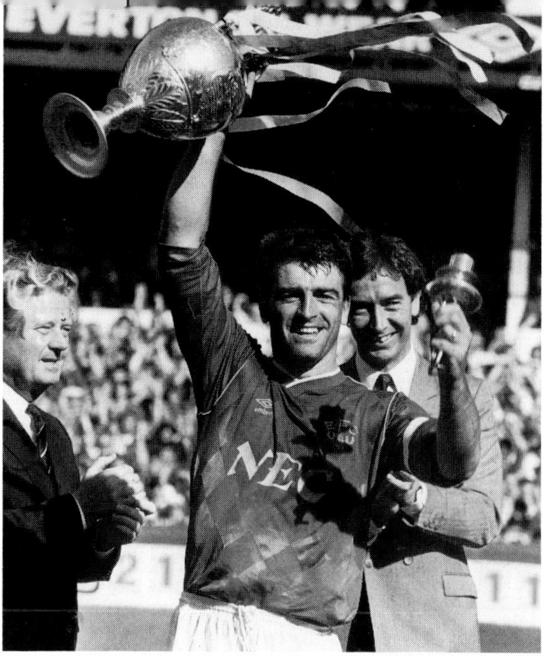

Displaying the 1987 Championship trophy to the Goodison faithful.

The centre-backs celebrating the 1987 Championship success. This time Howard Kendall had no complaints about Dave Watson having his hands on a bottle of champagne.

My best supporters, (from left to right) Dad's brother Graham, Mum, Dad, Sharon and Graham's wife Jo, celebrate the League Championship victory with the skipper.

Best Wishes Tommy
S. Ratcliffe.

steamed off into the sunset, but they were getting all the media build-up. It irritated but we were used to the hype surrounding that club. We accept it is in the nature of things where they're concerned. It doesn't matter if they're doing well or not. They just seem to be the 'in' club for people to talk about. Ever since the Munich disaster wrecked the Busby Babes they have had a sympathy vote. But hype and sympathy don't figure too highly on the list of necessities for winning titles. All they do is put more pressure on United and make the rest of us grit our teeth that bit harder.

We tested out what they'd got in the Charity Shield that year and we didn't have much trouble winning 2–0. That was the game I goaded my mate, Sheeds, into giving a performance worthy of his talent. He'd never done himself justice at Wembley and I was determined that was going to change.

'You haven't played at Wembley, have you, Sheeds?'

'Of course, I have.'

'No, I know you've been on the field there, but you haven't actually played, have you?'

Then I brought down a pillow and a blanket to the coach.

'What's that for?'

'For you. You might as well have them when you get out there.'

Well, the effect was tremendous. He shocked John Gidman, clattering him in the first minute. It's not something Giddy would have expected at all from Sheeds, who just went on from there. I've never seen him put in so many tackles or work as he did.

I felt we were in with a great chance of keeping our crown and United's great run didn't alter that. We were confident. The team hadn't changed, apart from Gary Lineker coming in. Our gut feeling about United was, 'they've got to crack and have a bad spell. Let's see how they react then.' We struck another blow at their morale when we won 4–2 at Old Trafford in the Super Cup, the competition dreamed up to make up for the European gates lost because of Heysel. That was their first defeat after eight straight wins. Just to rub it in, we beat them in the return at Goodison and then, more important, did it again in the League on Boxing Day, 3–1. By the time, two days later, Lineker had broken Wednesday – and won his personal battle with the fans – we were third, just three points adrift of United. Just about the only real setback we'd had was losing a League Cup replay against Chelsea after we'd held them at Stamford Bridge. All this time we'd been without the influence of Peter Reid because of achilles trouble and Derek Mountfield because of his knee cartilage. Thanks to the versatility of Pat Van den Hauwe, who had a brilliant spell at centre-half, Adrian Heath, Kevin Richardson, Alan Harper and Gary Stevens, we kept on going despite our problems. We finally hit the top in February when Reidy made a fairy-tale comeback after five months out, scoring the only goal against Spurs seven minutes from time. You couldn't fault his timing. And when we won 2–0 at Anfield, two games later, that seemed to be it.

The previous two times we'd won there we'd gone on to take the title and there was nothing in that game, or the way Liverpool were scraping results, to suggest we wouldn't do it again. It was a good performance and we got what we deserved; but in the end it did us more harm than good. That victory may have made us too comfortable, taking that vital edge off our play. If we'd lost, it would have made us grit our teeth and go grafting again. That's exactly what defeat did for Liverpool, besides making Kenny Dalglish have a drastic re-think on tactics. It was after that he chucked out the sweeper system he had used on and off and, from that moment, Liverpool never lost a game, winning eleven out of twelve. Our finish wasn't bad, two defeats out of twelve, but their consistency was incredible.

Even so, I felt bitter about the way we finally lost our crown at Oxford. We were denied two penalties; one blatant one when John Trewick fouled Kevin Richardson. You have to live with decisions and hope they even out over the nine months, but it's hard to take when you've slogged for something through forty games. It just wasn't our night. For some reason Links didn't have his lucky boots with him. They'd been kept together with a prayer and visits to the maker's boot 'hospital' because he'd been so successful with them and wouldn't let them 'die'. Even someone as laid back as Links had his little superstitions. Coincidence or not, he fired a rare blank that night and we were done. When we got back to the dressing-room, we heard Liverpool had won that night and knew everything we had worked for was gone.

Paul Bracewell gives me a twinge of conscience. I can't forget the hassle we gave him when he was in agony with his ankle injury – and we didn't believe him. It was at Newcastle on New Year's Day, 1986, when he and big Billy Whitehurst collided in a tackle which left Brace with a suspected broken leg. As it turned out, it would have been better for him if it had been broken. He wasn't the only casualty that day. Trevor Steven injured a foot and Kevin Sheedy his groin, leaving us with nine fit men. But for Brace it was the start of a nightmare when he must have feared he was going mad and he wasn't getting much help from his mates. The X-ray showed nothing. Examination showed nothing. He kept going, with a match off here and there, playing in nineteen of our final twenty-six matches, including the FA Cup final with Liverpool, and he was often brilliant. But every day he'd come in and say the pain was killing him.

Well, we just couldn't understand how anyone could play as well as he was and be in the kind of pain he said he was. I'm afraid that Reidy, who knows a thing or two about injuries and suffering, Sheeds, Adrian Heath and I gave him a few mouthfuls about it. He was getting comments like, 'Wish there was always something wrong with you if you can play like that.' But he kept saying the pain was unbearable and the stick got to him in the end. Maybe that's why he carried on so long because, knowing what we know now, you've just got to hand it to him for giving it a go as long as he did. Maybe it's no coincidence that he was born in the same place, Heswall, as that other survivor, Ian Botham. I remember particularly the Anfield derby, seven weeks after the Newcastle match. We learned later he was in absolute agony even during the pre-match kick-about, although again we did not realize it, and he couldn't go on after half-time. Yet he'd put in a tremendous amount of work during that half; he played great and never limped. It was a vital game and we were at him. 'What're you talking about, you can't go on? You've had a great half.' But the lad was near to tears and even his will broke this time.

That injury caused him a lot of mental pain as well as physical, not to mention the World Cup place in Mexico his performances had earned. It took eighteen months, five operations and an American specialist to pinpoint the problem, a piece of loose bone freakishly growing on the ankle. It meant a terrible chunk had been carved out of Brace's career – and it left a few red faces around Goodison. But it's when something like that happens you are reminded how precarious a career soccer can be. Maybe the average punter doesn't take that into account as much as he should when he has a go at players over the size of rewards they can get.

12

Final Flaws

Everton went into the 1986 FA Cup final ready to run through brick walls. It wasn't just the Cup that was at stake. For once in its history the old trophy was almost secondary. There was a greater motivation driving us – fear! Not of Liverpool, but of failure. We went into that unique all-Mersey FA Cup final knowing that we could finish a great season with nothing to show for it. Not only that, we stood between Liverpool and the rare double of League and Cup which, until ten days before, had been on the line for us. We were mentally right. We had prepared right, except for one crucial area, and we paid for it. We had a case for asking for a change of referee.

I do not say that lightly. The FA Cup final is almost as big an occasion for the whistler as it is for the player. It should be the peak of his career and I would hate to take that experience away from anyone. But, as with footballers, places and honours should go on merit, not sentiment. The fact is, unintentionally of course, we thought that Alan Robinson had given us a raw deal in the League Cup final against Liverpool two years before. His performance that day wasn't something that was going to inspire our confidence in him. It was an insensitive appointment. Referees have a tough time and it's important, especially on such an occasion that he should start with the confidence of both teams. I suppose there was a feeling that it couldn't happen again. But it did. He missed giving us another clear penalty when Stevie Nicol shoved Graeme Sharp in the back as he shaped for a free header in the first half. Again Mr Robinson may have been unsighted. He would have some cause for that because the ball was slanted forward towards Sharpy who was around the six-yard area, and Nicol was behind him. But experience and homework should have told the referee it was a foul. There was no way Nicol could have reached that ball fairly from his position and Sharpy, the best header of a ball in the game, was hardly going to act as if he was hit in the back when he's bang in front of goal like that. I don't blame Stevie for protecting his goal the best way he could, but he shouldn't have got away with it.

A goal then, followed by the one Gary Lineker scored from Peter Reid's brilliant fifty-yard ball, would have given us a good lead at half-time and I don't think we would have allowed Liverpool to come back from that. I remember going in at half-time and thinking 'that so-and-so's done us again', but I wasn't too bothered because we were going so well. I even had time for a laugh with Nicol in the tunnel. We had really got stuck into them, trying to get them riled up. And after I'd gone in hard on Jan Molby, I got involved with Nicol. I grabbed the ball to stop him taking the free kick fast. Then there was a bit of a shoving match which ended with me throwing the ball and catching him hard on the nose. Things quietened down a bit, but as we went down the tunnel at half-time, I felt a tap on the shoulder. I knew Stevie was behind me so I thought 'here we go. Trouble.' But as I turned round, ready for anything, there he was, grinning and saying through his nose in a funny voice, 'You see what you've done to my nose?' And I just cracked up.

After half-time it was Liverpool who looked like cracking up. They were all over the place in defence. I've never seen them in such a state. Bruce Grobbelaar actually punched Jim Beglin after a mix-up between them. Kenny was shouting and bawling. Everyone was arguing and I thought, 'We've got this wrapped up if we can get another one here. They've gone.' But we just couldn't make it stick. Bruce made a great save off Sharpy's brilliant header. Sheeds missed one and there were bits and pieces in the penalty area we couldn't profit from. At that time the only way they were going to get back into the game was if we allowed them. And that's just what happened. Gary Stevens had time to play a simple ball down the line which he would normally have done blindfold. This time he slightly underhit the ball in the long grass and we were caught by a sucker punch as we were moving out. Liverpool were doubly lucky in that Molby was hanging back instead of getting back to cover Reidy as we broke out. So, when we lost the ball, he was high and dry in a dangerous position and made the most of his luck, putting Rushy through for the equalizer.

From then on, they were lifted and things went badly for us, on and off the pitch. Craig Johnston made it 2–1 and it was then that Howard Kendall made the worst substitution decision of his time at Goodison. I'm not quarrelling with throwing on Adrian Heath. Where he went badly wrong was in taking off Gary Stevens. For once he seemed to have let emotion rule his brain. It didn't look as if it was done for tactical reasons but through disgust with Gary for giving the ball away. It was the worst thing he could have done to the player and to the team. Gary wasn't having the best of games but you don't do that to a player when he's just done something wrong, especially with him being so young. It left him totally shell-shocked, and that savage act cost Howard the use of a player aching to put right his mistake and, worse, left the team without its proper shape. If we'd kept that, we might have clawed our way back in. There's always a chance you might scrape one and go into extra time. When you get to that stage anything can happen. Trevor Steven hadn't done much that day and he could have gone to let in Adrian without affecting the balance of the team.

Instead, we were left with three at the back and one of them was Derek Mountfield who didn't start 100 per cent fit.

He'd only played after taking a morning fitness test. What with that and the effect of a long season and that heavy pitch, I've never felt so tired as I did in the last ten minutes. And we were so strung out all over the place that Reidy was heading balls away at centre-half. It wasn't surprising that Rushy made it 3–1. Nothing much was said afterwards. It was a time for saying nothing. There was just utter disappointment in the air, knowing we'd played so well for so long and then had just thrown it away. Maybe that's why Liverpool never got a lot of credit for what they did that year. I know that team wasn't as good as some they have had, but they had done the double. People still harp on now about the Tottenham and Arsenal double sides and how great they were. But after two days' chat about it in the papers, that was it. Over. I can't help feeling that if it had been Tottenham, Arsenal or Manchester United, we'd still be hearing about it now.

No Everton team must ever be put through the cruel, unnecessary ordeal we had to suffer after losing out on the double. Philip Carter and John Smith, the chairmen of Everton and Liverpool, may be wise in many ways but when they agreed both teams should travel back on the same plane and then follow each other round Liverpool in their coaches it showed an utter lack of sensitivity to the players' feelings in such a situation. These chairmen are men who love their clubs and their decisions are governed by that. I'm sure their action that time was done with good intentions – another gesture at giving a show of solidarity a year after Heysel. But if they had only thought a bit deeper they must have realized what they were asking and then thrown it out.

Both sides dreaded what would come after the final. The

thought of that journey was in our minds all the way to Wembley. I had talked it over with Jocky Hansen and we were united against it. Both of us realized how tough it would be on the losers. And, after talking to him, I just wondered whether Liverpool would have gone through with it if they had lost. Maybe you have to experience the bitterness to realize the depth of players' misery when they lose a Wembley final. It's not easy to get over. And this was no ordinary final to lose. What made it worse was that we hadn't just lost the Cup – we had handed it to them.

I was disappointed that Howard Kendall hadn't put his foot down before the idea had a chance to get off the ground. There is some excuse for the chairmen not being able to imagine what the players were being asked to do, but Howard knew exactly what was involved. Twice, he had been an FA Cup final loser, once as a seventeen-year-old. But when I approached him some weeks before the final, he said it had been agreed between the chairmen and he could do nothing about it. I left feeling it was sheer politics and the players were being asked to grit their teeth and get on with it. I would not like that to happen again – to anybody. And it won't as far as I'm concerned. We'd have to put a stop to it if it was ever suggested again or there would be a few going absent without leave. Only Reidy went missing that time. He had a possible move to Cologne on his mind and maybe thought he wouldn't be around to answer questions. Right or wrong, what he did summed up everybody's feelings. I know I was in two minds about going. If I hadn't been skipper I don't think I would have gone.

The day was everything we feared, worse than actually losing the final. We'd had a surprisingly good 'do' on the Saturday night considering what had happened. All the families were there and the lads were great the way they went about trying to forget about the awful afternoon. Then came the morning after and hangovers were the last things on our minds. It wasn't very nice to be at the airport to see the Liverpool lads come in all happy after the night before. They were a little bit drunk whereas we'd sobered up by that time. Just watching them was enough to do that. But there was no awkwardness when we chatted to them in the lounge. Lads like Steve McMahon and Rushy aren't the sort to dwell on what's happened. To give Liverpool their due, they were as embarrassed as we would have been about travelling on the same plane.

That journey round Liverpool must have taken two hours but it seemed like four! And we gradually developed a problem which even took over from the other misery. When you've had a few drinks, two hours is a long time to be on a bus with no toilet. We were growing desperate by the time we were crawling down Queen's Drive. We thought we might just hold on, but then a bus shelter suddenly collapsed under the weight of fans. An ambulance was called, a traffic jam built up and we were stuck solid. We groaned and crossed our legs a bit tighter. No use. Finally, someone broke. He saw a sympathetic-looking woman standing in her doorway, leapt out of the bus, plunged through the supporters and begged the use of her toilet. At that moment she could have asked any price and got it.

The next thing, there were about twenty players hurtling up her stairs, holding themselves in and desperately hoping they weren't going to make a mess of her hospitality. At the height of the frenzy, in walked her husband, who happened to be a Liverpool supporter and wasn't very amused to find himself playing host to the enemy. 'What the hell's going on here?' he shouted, and didn't sound satisfied enough with 'we're only using your toilet, mate', to start thinking about putting up a plaque to mark the visit. That was just about the only funny part of the day. I know I couldn't wait for it to end so I could just get in the car and go home. That defeat was worse for me than even losing the World Cup finals chance against Scotland.

Wales' set-up is the nearest thing to a club you are likely to get on the international scene, but they are still people you meet occasionally. When its Everton, it involves people you live with and train with day in, day out. That's what made the pain greater – and that bus ride only drove the knife deeper.

13

Second Time Around

They say love is sweeter the second time around. I wouldn't know about that but our second championship in three years certainly gave me even more satisfaction than when we ended that fifteen-year drought in 1985. If ever there was a triumph for squad strength, more shrewd sometimes inspired buying, and sheer spirit, it was this one in 1987. I do not believe there have been any title winners in the history of the championship who have had to play so much of their winning campaign without five internationals. And we'd lost Gary Lineker. Bad injuries, plus a 1,000–1 infection, meant we kicked off without Neville Southall, Gary Stevens, Pat Van den Hauwe, Peter Reid and Paul Bracewell. Another, Kevin Sheedy, went through the season at probably no more than eighty per cent efficiency, nursing knee trouble that would have probably been given surgery earlier but for the extent of our troubles. And nearly half the campaign had gone before a seventh, Dave Watson, really understood the system and played to his full potential.

Replacing Links' forty goals turned out to be the least of our worries. When you think about it, most teams would have been crippled just having to do without Reidy and Brace.

Brace, half of the game's best engine room, missed the whole season while he had what seemed like operation after operation on his ankle. The other half, Reidy, did not play a full game until January because of a stress fracture picked up in the Mexico World Cup, and was never at full power until almost at the death. England's best right-back, Gary Stevens, also injured in Mexico, was out until December. Neville, the world's top keeper, missed the first sixteen games while he rebuilt muscles after the terrible damage done to his ankle ligaments five months before in Dublin. And the formidable Pat Van den Hauwe was hit so badly by a blood infection on the pre-season tour that he did not return until the same day as Reidy. Pat's absence sparked more rumours than the average royal romance. You name it, he was supposed to have caught it. He knew from the amount of stick he took that the lads didn't take the stories seriously. It's when they are quiet about such things that you start getting worried! It means they suspect the rumours might be true.

Whatever the bug was, it hit him hard. And it was sudden. We were in Holland ready for the next stage of the pre-season trip to Germany when it struck. We went out for a few drinks one night and he was fine when we got back to the hotel. But by the time we got up next morning he was on his way home. He had woken in the night, screaming with pain. His ankle had blown up to three times its normal size. He made an SOS call to physio John Clinkard who dosed him with sedatives to knock him out. Then he was shipped off to hospital, given drugs and had to give the ankle complete rest. The whole thing really knocked him about.

If all this injury and infection was not enough, we had the little matter of a fired-up Rushy desperate to leave Liverpool with another trophy in the cabinet. So, all in all, it wasn't surprising that Liverpool were favourites. Given our handicaps, we ought to have been tipped to go down. Yet we finished up nine points ahead of them – though it always felt a lot closer than that. It's a miracle that isn't hard to explain. Rushy may have been fired up, but there was across Stanley Park a whole club bursting its gut to take that title. No money could give the motivation we had that year. Nor did Howard Kendall need to reach for any inspiration until the run-in. Pride and revenge, in that order, were our driving forces. We were still burning over Liverpool doing the double which should have been ours. The bitter feeling was that they hadn't so much won it, as we had lost it. It was a hurt that got down into the core of the club. After that nightmare coach ride following the Cup Final, all we had wanted was to get away and re-charge. Reidy, Gary, Trevor and Graeme Sharp had the World Cup finals to take their minds off that double disaster. The rest of us did it in Magaluf. It was a time just to be with the lads and break the drinking record. I think we managed it. It was a long week but it was much needed and we came back better for it. It wasn't just the beer and sun that got us going again. We'd also had a terrific boost when the boss told me in Majorca that he wouldn't be following Links to Barcelona. I had to ask because there had been plenty of speculation about him going since the turn of the year and he'd taken some stick from the lads. It was, 'Si, si, Senor Kendall' when he asked for something and, 'How do you like your paella, Senor Howard?' He had taken it all pretty well but there was some embarrassment because the stories had some strength to them. I don't believe it had anything to do with his decision, but I believe he realized on that holiday the mood of the lads. That we wanted to prove we were the best in the land. When a team feels like that, a manager doesn't want to be somewhere else and none of us wanted him to go. It might have hit the terrific spirit that had built up if he had deserted us. So, by the time I'd had the family holiday with Sharon and the kids, I was absolutely itching to kick a ball again and make someone suffer – preferably, Liverpool.

It was the year of the super stand-ins. It had to be with the number of gaps we had to fill. And of those deputies, two stood out, Paul Power and Alan Harper. Paul was far from being Howard's biggest buy, but he wasn't far off being the best. He cost £65,000 and there were people around at the time who thought that pricey; but he turned out to be priceless to us. He was nearly thirty-three when he came to Goodison. The only club he'd ever known was Manchester City and for many years he seemed to be involved in a struggle for survival. He was past the stage when he dreamed he could go up the ladder. At that age, the usual route is different. But he finished up with a championship medal and no one earned it more. When he came, all he expected to be was a squad player, a shadow for anyone down the left side. As it worked out, he made his debut against Liverpool in the Charity Shield and never missed a game until the final stages when a knee injury picked up after Christmas, forced him out. It was a real feat.

He started at left-back because Pat was ill. When Sheeds went down injured, he shifted into midfield. And when Sheeds came back, Paul moved into the centre because we were short there. He did a good job wherever he was asked and scored vital goals. There's evidence enough to convince you that he's no geriatric. He's a great athlete, fitter than most people at the club, and a true professional who turns in good performances week in, week out. Above all, he wants to win. In short, an Evertonian in all but upbringing. Yet, when he came, the fans were calling him all sorts of names. 'Why have you come here, you silly old bastard?' was among the politer questions. All that was a relic of longstanding unfriendliness between Everton and City fans. Long before the end of the campaign I think they knew why he'd come. But he seems to be one of those wholehearted players who is never fully appreciated by the fans. For instance, no one wore an Everton shirt with greater pride or heart than Terry Darracott but he used to take some flak.

Paul had pulled his guts out for City in around 400 games

yet the fans responded to his testimonial match against us with a miserable 7,000 gate. It could have been better for him if Manchester United had been in the other corner instead of us and twice he felt they let him down. It seems that these days people will only turn out for such games if they are attracted by the opposition, not because of the fella's service to the club. We didn't do him any favours on the night, beating City 4–1. I don't think we played better all year.

As for Harpo, it was the year he came into his own. He'd got so frustrated as a bit player that he must have come close to the record for being the most weeks on a weekly contract. He'd been on one for around eighteen months. Howard valued him highly and kept tempting him to sign for a long-term contract but Harpo was desperate for first-team football. He'd have been a bargain for somebody but, amazingly, the only club that came in for him hard was Villa – and he was injured the day before he was due to finalize the deal with Graham Turner, then Villa's boss. It was near the transfer deadline and Turner was in trouble. He couldn't wait for Harpo and so signed Andy Blair and Steve Hunt.

Harpo never got another look-in there and I don't know who was unluckier, Villa or him. But I know how thankful we are that he stayed. In the 1986/7 campaign, he filled six different shirts, just about as many positions, and grew in assurance the more he became a part of the team. The fans had given him a bad time when he came. In fact, he was getting stick from all angles. He comes from a family of dyed-in-the-wool Liverpudlians and they couldn't believe it when he changed sides. There were even calls of 'traitor' at his wedding. I don't know about the family, but he certainly won Evertonians over. And so they should have been converted. He's a helluva skilful player who shows that Mark Lawrenson is not the only one around who can do a job all over the park. Yet he began that season with his main incentive being to play well enough to tempt someone to get him away.

He couldn't see any way past Gary Stevens for the spot he really wanted, right-back. And all he wanted was to play regularly, the basic wish of any professional. Although that's a bit ironic considering he's played almost as many League games for Everton as Reidy. It was half way through the year before he decided his stand had gone on long enough and signed a long contract. That seemed to gee him up even more. Some people go the other way when they get a bit of security and ease down. But it gave him a new lease of life. And it was harsh on him when eventually he had to give way to Gary. When Gary is on form he is the better right-back, but at that time he was struggling to get his touch back after Mexico and that injury. Harpo was playing the better, but it was Howard's way to choose what he thought were his best players, no matter how well the stand-in had done.

He has a faith and belief in pedigree and quality which can be heartbreaking for deputies. It was that way of doing things which upset Bobby Mimms. He did nothing wrong as Neville Southall's deputy but was out as soon as Nev was fit. Bobby reckoned if you did the job well, you should keep it no matter who you're keeping out. But I would argue his is a different case. True, Bob had never let us down and we were confident that he wouldn't, but there is a difference when you've got the best keeper in the world behind you. You just expect him to make saves. When he doesn't there are questions asked.

Replacing goals can be a lot more difficult than replacing bodies. And, on the face of it, making up Links' massive total was asking a lot. But I wasn't worried. We had every confidence in Adrian Heath and Graeme Sharp. Their partnership can be almost telepathic. We also remembered that although Gary had a great season with us, we had won nothing with his goals.

This was the time when Paul Wikinson could have come into his own, but didn't. His big chance was there but he couldn't take it. I was disappointed he didn't give more. Great lad, but too placid and easy going. No one was more laid back than Links, but he did the business out on the park. I would have liked to see Wilky lose his temper more in a game. He could have been a real handful then. I've seen him spark once or twice when he's been hit in training. He can be a nasty fella and if he could get that little bit of devil in his game, he'd be some player. Too often he seemed to be in another world. For instance, when a few of the lads start living in the same area, they get together and take it in turns to drive the others to training. Wilky did it one day, good as gold, but when the session was over and the lads were looking for their lift back, he turned round and said, 'Sorry, I can't. Didn't I tell you I was going back to Grimsby to see my mum and dad?' So they were left cursing and stranded. Wilky also bought a second floor flat with no lift – just when a baby was due!

It would be silly to say we wouldn't miss Links, especially away from home, where his tremendous pace could hit people on the break. We always felt dangerous with him there. All we needed was just one break, with most teams playing flat at the back. It might only be a hopeful ball but he'd capitalize on it. Sometimes we seemed to rely on him too much. What we had to remember was that the year before he came, goals were coming from everywhere. We had to get back to that and adapt our style. There was no point in playing the quick ball over the top. Openings had to be worked, the responsibility of scoring had to be shared. And that's what happened.

Ask the average punter what it takes to be a successful professional footballer and he'll probably list skill, pace, courage and commitment. But these won't mean too much without something else. Character. Bottle. Self-belief. Call it what you will, but if you haven't got enough of it, you're in trouble. I'm talking about having the bloody-minded determination to get you through to your personal target, no matter what. It's the main reason why the careers of Dave Watson and Kevin Langley went different ways at Goodison. Dave is almost made of it, Kevin didn't show enough. The crowd broke Langley when the going got tough, but they couldn't break Watson, despite putting him through hell and back. Dave did have one big advantage. When he came from Norwich, he was already a full England international with all that means in terms of experience. Kevin came straight from the Third Division and was asked to do a massive job, but I believe Dave would have come through even if their circumstances had been switched.

Don't get me wrong. I still believe Langley is going to be a helluva player. He showed it when he came back to Goodison with Manchester City and his painful experience at Everton will probably do him good and make him harder mentally. All he lacked otherwise was pace and sometimes he looked a bit frightened of getting stuck in. He had composure and looked good in the pre–1986 season tour. But, coming from Wigan to cover for injured high-class midfielders like Peter Reid and Paul Bracewell, was asking a bit much. It was a great responsibility for the lad. If he could have been dropped after four or five games and taken away from the big pressure for a while, he could have been some Everton player. But, because of injuries, he was the best we had for that position and he had to stay with it. When he started to struggle, the crowd got to him and eventually broke him. His spirit went. He was frightened to have the ball and to do the things he'd been doing magnificently in the pre-season. Howard Kendall tried different things to revive him, but it was too late and I felt sorry for the lad. Even so, Langley's problem was slight compared with Watson's.

The big man had three heavy crosses to bear. He'd played for Liverpool, had never played in a system like ours and, worst, had replaced a terrace hero in Derek Mountfield. Any one of those would have been tough to take. Together, they were sheer torture. While I've been here, David Johnson, Kevin Sheedy and Alan Harper have all had to suffer the average Everton fan's instinctive reaction to an arrival from Anfield. It's a natural reaction. The day it changes, that special feeling between Everton and Liverpool will have gone. Only Jonno of those three didn't break through the acceptance barrier – and he'd started off as an Evertonian! Sheeds was hurt by it but is now one of their heroes. And no one gets a louder cheer than Harpo. But for Dave, the process was made longer and more agonizing because of the other handicaps.

The fans just couldn't see why Howard had paid nearly £1million for a centre-half when Derek Mountfield was there. Derek is an Evertonian to the soles of his boots. He had been a terrace fan and the fans related to him as one of their own. He was their idol and he had played a mighty part in our 1985 championship win, including the terrific bonus of ten goals – an incredible number for a centre-half who didn't even take penalties. There was also a suspicion among supporters that Howard had paid the money for Dave as a kind of sop to them after selling Gary Lineker to Barcelona. It was nothing of the kind. The fact was that Derek had knee trouble which, in Howard's eyes, made him suspect. It provoked a rare instance of Howard taking me into his confidence, presumably because it concerned something that directly affected me. Howard told me he couldn't take a chance with Derek because of fears he might break down. And if he was to sign someone, it couldn't just be a £100,000 stand-by because we had to win something after narrowly missing out the previous season.

He wanted a really good centre-half and asked me about Terry Butcher. I replied, 'Great player, but if you're going to get him, it'll have to be now because it looks like he's going to Manchester United or Rangers.' Howard agreed saying, 'I think he's a great player, too, and everyone is telling me to get him.' But he was bothered that it meant having two left-footers together in the heart of the defence. It had worked well enough when Mark Higgins and I were together. Our partnership had been good and effective and I've never understood why two left-footers should be thought any more of a handicap than having two right-footers linked. However, finally it was Dave who came. I was pleased. I knew he was someone who would go out there and give 110 per cent. Gary Stevens, Peter Reid and Paul Bracewell told me he was the sort of player who got stuck in even in England squad sessions. But our style of defence just floored him.

I've been there since it started so I'm used to it, but coming into it fresh is hard. He had been used to having a tight marking job on one specific opponent at Norwich. Show him a fella with a number nine on his back and he would stick to him, come what may. It's a game he liked, understood and it suited him. But that's not the way we do it. The number nine is taken by whoever is in his area. Dave would say to me before games 'keep talking to me, keep talking to me'. I did but he was continually being caught in two minds and I had to concentrate on helping him, covering for him more than I would have liked for my own game's sake.

To make it worse, the crowd were happy when he had a bad game. They felt they'd been proved right and the manager wrong. There were banners up for Derek. They shouted for him if they saw him on the bench and booed Dave. It also didn't help that Dave missed chances at the other end – the sort that Derek had been getting. Dave is built like a Roman gladiator. When he strips off, it makes us want to cover up. But it was his mental toughness that was even more impressive. He never let on that he was hurt. He even cracked jokes about it. But he was hurt. It finally showed when he did turn the corner. When the fans at last started chanting his name, he was very reluctant to give them a wave in acknowledgement.

The boss let him battle through it although he must have been tempted to take him out of the firing line for a while. He knew Dave had the character to survive the crisis and the players, especially, knew he would come through. The way he was training said everything. The only thing letting him down was our system. Everything else in his game was great. His heading was spot on and his tackling and will-to-win were still strong. It was just a positional thing and a matter of time before he got it right. In fact, it took him until Christmas, and I'm convinced it was an injury which helped him over that last barrier.

He damaged a hamstring at Southampton and had to sit out eight games. Those proved very important to him because he learned just by watching the way the team played. When he did return, the penny had just about dropped. Dave finished up having a great season in the 1986/7 title win. I'm not just saying that out of loyalty. I always thought Higgy was my ideal partner, but now if I had to make the choice it would be Dave. He goes into tackles that shouldn't be his to win. The fans have been won over. They realize he's a wholehearted player, a winner who wants only to play for Everton. But I believe the experience he suffered in that first season would have crushed him if he wasn't the character he is.

Despite all our problems we were always around the top of the Division and by the end of the Christmas holidays we had made the doubters sit up and think again. We went into the holiday fourth, some nine points adrift of Arsenal, but, by the time the New Year matches were out of the way, we'd had five successive wins, including one on QPR's plastic, and the Gunners were looking over their shoulders. We'd also had a massive boost when Ian Snodin turned down Liverpool in favour of us, saying he thought he'd have a better chance of winning things at Goodison. Bill Shankly must have twitched in his grave. It was only a matter of time before we took over.

When we went into the League Cup quarter-final with Liverpool, they were struggling for results and we were favourites to put them out. We were going well until poor Jim Beglin and Gary Stevens challenged hard for a 50–50 ball and the Irishman suffered a badly broken leg that was to put him out the rest of the season and more. Kenny Dalglish and

Ronnie Moran made an issue of it in the heat of the moment, pointing fingers at players, and Howard was angered by the Liverpool management's reaction. If they'd known Gary deep down, they would have realized they were wrong. He's not got one bit of a mean streak in him. Sometimes I think he's too nice to be a footballer. The tackle wasn't bad. There's no way he'd go into a tackle to hurt. If anything, he lacks that little bit of nastiness that defenders need and sometimes people take advantage of him. He could do with a little anger in his play. Many worse tackles than his were delivered that night, especially after the incident, and people just got up and walked away.

In fact, Gary's tackle was so ordinary, I didn't realize anything was wrong until I saw Sheeds and Steve McMahon running to get the ref's attention. The result was terrible for Jim, but Gary wasn't unscathed. It affected him not only in that match but in a few afterwards. It was the last thing he needed after being out half the season through injury. He'd found it a struggle getting back to the peak he hit before the Mexico World Cup, when he was so strong in defending and attacking that there was no one else around to touch him. His control, which once had been laughable, became brilliant almost overnight. He did visit Jim in hospital and, looking back, I wish more of us had. Sheeds, who was a mate was going to go but within four days was in hospital himself for a cartilage operation. As to the game, it was the team which had suffered the loss that raised themselves, which often happens. We lost composure and couldn't capitalize. Liverpool were both upset and inspired, and Rushy stole the only goal.

There are plenty of reasons why we took the 1987 championship, but I'll give you one which won't be found in the reference books and certainly not in the coaching manuals – a Chinese pick-me-up! I'm not joking. Without that we might never have achieved what we did. There was some talk that we used Royal Bee jelly to help us on the run-in. That's new to me. I never saw any of that honey stuff. No, it was going for a Chinese meal that gave us a real buzz! Losing the League Cup quarter-final to Liverpool had seemed to throw us off our stride for a time. We lost at Forest in a television game when we had a lot of chances. And though we did well to keep a hold of the FA Cup, 1–0 on the ice at Bradford where Peter Reid and Pat Van den Hauwe made terrific returns and Ian Snodin scored a fine goal, we didn't last much longer. In the fifth round, Wimbledon stopped us, 3–1, again in a televised match.

That was a bitter disappointment. We had grown to like Wembley rather a lot. We hadn't known what it was like to lose an FA Cup outside the twin towers since Manchester United had beaten us with an injury-time goal at Old Trafford in 1983. It was a habit we didn't fancy losing and we didn't see much to frighten us if we got past Wimbledon. Their strengths weren't secret or subtle – 100 per cent battling to make up for skill deficiency and making sure they got the most out of the aggression and air power of John Fashanu. But as Alan Cork, another of their strikers, had said after we had turned them over 3–0 at Goodison, 'The difference between Everton and most of the others is that they can scuffle when they have to.' Well, we didn't do enough scuffling that day. We had already won down there, 2–1, back in September, knocking them off the top of the League. But that time, because of our injury problems, Derek Mountfield had been slotted in with Dave Watson and me, giving us an extra centre-back to counter their big men in the penalty area. The tactic had worked well, but this time we used our normal system. For twenty minutes, we looked in a different class. Paul Wilkinson scored an early goal and we could have had more. But Gary Stevens gave away a silly penalty for a foul on Fashanu just before half-time and after that we were out-fought, which is a rare experience for us.

The sight was enough to make Howard Kendall decide it

was time for one of his Chinese pick-me-ups. These used to happen once or twice a year if he felt morale was slipping or that we were getting lackadaisical. He would take us off to a Chinese restaurant for a meal and a few drinks. Good things came out of those get-togethers and, in this case, it was the championship. It's a time for getting a few things off your chest and maybe telling the manager something you wouldn't unless you'd had some drink inside you. It was something that seemed to get everybody going again. The boss had given us a choice that time – a couple of days at The Belfry golf course down in the Midlands, or the meal. He wanted us to decide because it was important on these occasions that everybody should be there. All or nothing.

Reidy, who was still struggling for sharpness, said he wanted to improve his match fitness in the reserves. One or two others decided the same. So it was the Chinese. These events always start with a scramble. Nobody wants to sit next to the boss. In Howard's case, it wasn't a question of BO, but of earache! Besides looking after his wine glass, you had to suffer a succession of jokes which were pretty funny on the first hearing but not so funny on the twenty-first. The thing was to get a new boy alongside him. That time it was Dave Watson. After the meal we had some bottles of champagne, although we didn't exactly deserve them after the performance at Wimbledon. The boss ordered six, put five on the table and one between his feet. Then began the big wind-up. We'd start Howard off on one of his stories with something like 'you remember that time, boss, when. . .' and away he'd go, bending Dave's ear for twenty minutes while we got on with enjoying ourselves. When that story finished, we'd say 'oh, and what about the time. . .' and set him off again.

Dave was on his best behaviour because all this was new to him. He would nod and smile in the right places, but his head was probably ringing. Even so, he had the last word, brilliantly. When the lads offered Howard some champagne, the boss said, 'No, I'm all right, lads. I've got my bottle here. When all you lot have gone home, I'm going to have it quietly by the fire.' Then our champagne ran out and the restaurant had no more. So it's 'Come on, boss, let's have a drink of yours.' And we kept at him until eventually he gave in, grabbed the bottle he'd kept so carefully between his feet – and found it was empty. Dave had somehow worked a switch. I think you can say that would have been the last time he'd have sat next to Howard even if the boss hadn't gone to Bilbao.

That session certainly put the bubble back into us at just the right time. We needed everyone working for one another in the next match – Manchester United, at Old Trafford. That's hard at any time, but this was a particularly vital game and our objective had to be to make sure we didn't lose. We knew if we did that it could have been the end of our season. Usually, we had the Cups to fall back on. This time it was the League or nothing! We made sure we didn't lose. And that draw set us up for the final surge. We lost only twice more – once in another TV horror at Watford, and then when Ian Rush beat us almost single-handed at Anfield in Liverpool's last fling.

Mind you, if we'd appeared any more on the box I don't know what would have happened. We had this little feeling that if we played on a Sunday we would lose. We had no confidence in those games. None of the lads liked playing on that day. It wasn't a matter of religion and it may sound ridiculous for a hard-nosed professional to say so, but there was a feeling, no more than that, that we were playing on the wrong day of the week. For instance, it was odd to pick up a Sunday paper and read about everybody else's matches when we still had to go into action. The week is geared for a Saturday game and we never got over that feeling although Howard Kendall tried to avoid it by delaying our usual preparation by a day to keep us in the same sort of routine.

The Watford game wasn't the happiest for Wayne Clarke to make his debut. In the first half, we played some great stuff, but fell away and defeat cost us the lead in the title race. We needed Clarkie. The boss bought him from Birmingham because Graeme Sharp had damaged an ankle and couldn't come back until the game we clinched the championship at Norwich. Clarkie, an uncanny lookalike for brother Allan, the old England striker, was a tonic. He is out of a completely different mould to Sharpy. He's not the quickest, or most brilliant in the air, but he's got a good touch, tremendous self-confidence, and he scored some vital goals. That confidence showed with his first strike for us, a nerveless thirty-yard chip at Arsenal after keeper John Lukic had mis-kicked. He might have been delivering it in practice, it was so cool. It was also the only goal of that Highbury game, killing off what was left of Arsenal's challenge, and putting us within three points of Liverpool, who had unbelievably lost at home to Wimbledon.

That Arsenal result was one of seven successive wins when we conceded only two goals. A crucial run. Any team that's going to win the League needs to put such a run together and there's no better time to do it than on the run-in. Included in that series of wins was a great 2–1 result at Chelsea, a team that had never brought us much luck. Alan Harper hit a screamer from twenty-five yards, then hit the bar from thirty, and was promptly tagged 'Zico'. It was a big win and our determination to get it was outstanding even for us. You'll understand how outstanding when I tell you that we lost Sheeds half way through, injured again. By the time we went to Anfield, we were six points in front with a game in hand. We were confident and played like it. Liverpool did a Spurs on us, paying us the compliment of sticking five in midfield. We both did justice to the occasion, starting with two great strikes by Steve McMahon and Sheeds. They set the tone for a match that was tailor-made for Rushy. He needed two goals to match Dixie Dean's 19-goal Mersey derby record and naturally, in the way he kept scoring against us, got them. But anyone there will tell you that the 3–1 result was harsh. People said they couldn't remember seeing Liverpool penned back in their own half for as long as we had them there in the second half. But we couldn't make it stick, and when they broke it was the old story of great finishing by Rushy.

Despite Sheeds' superb free-kick goal, he wasn't right with his knee. He'd come back a little too early, which he seems to have done a few times. But that eagerness is understandable. It's something that reflects the determination of the whole squad not to miss a chance of getting into the team, especially when honours are being played for. Sheeds didn't play again in the last four matches. He is very important to us, but even after the derby we didn't feel we would lose the Championship. We were just one win away. The only time there was a little worry during that final sprint was when we failed to wrap up the title in the next game.

Manchester City were virtually doomed to relegation when they came to Goodison, but we could not put them away. Kev Langley, who was on loan to them by that time, showed the fans who had helped frighten him out of his Everton career what a good player he was. He realized he wasn't going to come back and if he wanted to make a point, he did. The whole team responded to him and they caused us problems. Maybe because the pressure had been lifted with their fate almost decided, they had all the confidence in the world and certainly didn't look like a bottom-of-the-table side who hadn't won away all season. We finished up 0–0, and choked! Just to make our day, Wayne Clarke dislocated a shoulder in the last minute. The one great consolation was that Liverpool had gone down to Coventry, but the lads still began to fear we had let it slip because, two days later, we were at Norwich, a place where we didn't have the best of records.

The supporters didn't seem to fancy it, either. There were about 7,000 there and I expected more for a potentially big occasion like that. But, of course, because of the way football is we had the title won within two minutes – and via one of the unlikeliest boots on the field. Pat Van den Hauwe had only scored twice in his career up to then, but if the net hadn't been there to stop it, his shot would probably still be going. It was especially great for him after all the ridiculous stories that had gone around after his illness. In a way, relief was as big a feeling as triumph on that night. I don't think I realized how much it had taken out of me until we were on the way home. I didn't feel too good. I just flopped out on the back seat of the coach and fell asleep, absolutely exhausted. Not even Terry Darracott's 'Champions' Radio' routine could keep me awake – and that's saying something!

There was plenty to remember that campaign for, not least the finale. On the face of it, everything was set up for a good day. There were 44,000 in the sun at Goodison waiting to salute the squad's marvellous effort and see me lift the old League Championship trophy. And it was a great feeling to get hold of that historic cup which, for some reason, had been shamefully stashed away in the League's cellar when sponsorship took over. England manager Bobby Robson presented that award for our nine months' slog and I felt so good. But after that it was sheer, ugly anti-climax. And that was Luton's fault. They ought to have been just the team to make it a good finish. The pressure was off. They'd had a good season and they could play a bit. The setting was right for us all just to go out there and show ourselves off. But Luton had other, nastier ideas. They just did not want us to enjoy our day. We'd had a few 'spats' with them in the past, the last in December at Kenilworth Road. We lost there, 1–0. Steve Foster was sent off and Graeme Sharp collected a booking which meant suspension.

They started putting themselves about, leaving the foot in. Mike Newell, especially, seemed to be having a go. Being a frustrated Liverpudlian perhaps he felt a bit of hurt at our taking the title from them. Whatever the reason, what followed was an affair which included a punch-up, a sending-off, two penalties and too many niggles. They also scored first when Mark Stein shot in from twenty yards. Well, we had both penalties, one of them dubious, put away by Trevor Steven. Peter Nicholas was sent off for going in on Reidy.

It was all utterly senseless and pointless. Nothing they did could take away from the fact that we had won again the greatest prize in our football. But what a sour finish. I can only put it down to some kind of jealousy on their part. Why, I don't know. They should have been celebrating. After all, they are a club with little tradition and small gates, yet their plastic excuse for a pitch had helped them to reach the highest place in their history. Pity they couldn't have taken some satisfaction from that rather than trying to spoil Everton's celebration.

14

Farewell Howard

I was shocked when Howard Kendall left. Not because he'd gone, but because of where he'd gone. The thinking was that if he left Everton it would be for one of Europe's big boys. Terry Venables had recommended him to Barcelona; Athletico Madrid and Juventus were in the frame. Had he left for any of those we'd have understood better. I was in Barbados when the news broke, about four days after he'd left. I was a bit off-hand about it when someone said, 'I see Howard's gone abroad.' But when he said it was Athletic Bilbao, that stumped me. I wouldn't have thought they had a cat in hell's chance. OK, it's a club with tradition but with a built-in handicap, the Basque-only rule. There are enough problems getting used to a new language, a new country and, virtually, a new game, without that extra one.

He'd said nothing to me about going, but then we weren't that close and I wouldn't have expected him to tell me. I had talked to him generally about the future when we were on the final part of the team's holiday trip in Hawaii. There was plenty of speculation about him at the time because he'd been hedging about signing a new contract the club were pushing at him. All he told me then was that there were a few things concerning his contract he had to iron out with chairman Philip Carter. Judging by what he said then, I thought he would stay if the chairman offered him what he wanted. But I gather it was on that trip that he told Mick Heaton he was going. Nobody blamed him, especially if he'd been offered ridiculous amounts of money. It must have been some offer to prise him away, but he'd won all he could for Everton. Just about the only thing he hadn't won was the European Cup and the fact that he couldn't even have a shot at it after Heysel was a bitter frustration.

It was the one thing that was missing and our Cup Winners Cup glory had made his hunger even greater. That was almost certainly a big factor in his decision. If we had been allowed back into Europe in 1987 he would have stayed with us. I'm certain of that. I had never sensed he was getting restless, although when your name is mentioned in the same breath as Barcelona and Juventus it would be enough to unsettle anyone! I'd had my battles with him, but the only lads who wouldn't have been sorry to see him go were those who weren't getting a game, or those he'd pushed out.

You do feel sorry for the likes of Alan Harper and Kevin Richardson, good players who'd come in, played well as deputies and then got left out. They had their ups and downs with him but, deep down they thought he was a good manager. He understood their frustration but he would only take so much. If he felt they were getting out of hand, he would fire off a cutting remark that would hurt them. He had a sharp mind and his tongue wasn't far behind when he felt it necessary.

He was a player's man. He never lost sight of what made us tick. I liked the way he would make sure injured players, especially the long-term ones, were never allowed to feel out of things. He made sure they were kept involved, always taking them on away trips. The thing that disappointed me as captain was that he didn't have as many heart-to-heart talks with me as I would have liked. There were times when things weren't going well that he could have done with opinions from the dressing-room. Maybe he didn't think them worth having, or thought he had enough from the 'brains trust' upstairs. I found, when he did talk to me, that he sometimes wanted information that could have put me in a very awkward position. He might ask me if there was something the matter with a certain player. I told him that it was up to him to ask the lad concerned. I didn't want to be regarded as some kind of spy in the dressing- room. I was a player, too, and I could see the lads getting very uneasy if they thought I was talking behind their backs. I wasn't that type, and I think Howard realized it.

The way he left showed his class. He didn't make a big thing of saying goodbye to everyone. He said it was Colin's show and he didn't want to do anything that might interfere with that. He just wrote me a letter asking me to 'thank the lads for everything they've done for me' and wishing us every success. I phoned to thank him.

He did come in quietly to pick up a few things while we were in pre-season training. Colin came down and said to me, 'The boss (I guess old habits die hard) is upstairs if you want to have a word.' So I went up and had about five minutes before we started training again. But he never called us together and that was right. You might start crying or something! He wasn't the only one leaving. Mick Heaton also decided it was time to go. In a way it was fitting. They had come to the club together. Now they were leaving at the same time, even if it couldn't be to Bilbao because of their Basque-only rule. I think it was a matter of frustration for Mick. He had been getting further and further from the coaching side and into the backroom. He, too, never let slip he was leaving. We never saw him to say goodbye. Maybe it would have been too much for him, but he'd been a part of the rise out of trouble and it could have ended better.

My main worry about Howard Kendall's leaving was not how we would get along without him, but who would replace him. I was desperately afraid the board might go outside the club for a 'name', although it wouldn't have bothered me so much if they had gone for Brian Clough. That might surprise some, knowing the man's reputation for doing things his way and remembering the upset he caused at another well-established set-up at Leeds. He lasted forty-four days! But Cloughie and Howard have similar ideas about training and I don't think he would have seen much to change. No, what troubled me was the thought of someone like Howard Wilkinson or Graham Taylor taking charge. I mean no disrespect to either. They've had their minor successes in their own particular ways. But their ways and methods are far from ours and we've seen nothing in them to make us jealous.

Andy Gray used to scornfully break down Sheffield Wednesday's method as 'aiming the ball for the corner flags, piling bodies after it and hoping they'll force something from set pieces'. That just about summed it up. It wasn't football as we know it at Everton and, whatever the fashionable FA coaching theory about the efficiency of blasting the ball from back to front as fast as possible, I can't imagine that frantic, helter-skelter style ever being accepted at the old 'school of science.' If you're going to reduce the game to that, you might as well produce super goalkeepers who could spend all day kicking the ball at each other.

We also didn't relish the kind of training that apparently goes with that style of football and I believe either Wilkinson or Taylor would have changed our whole training structure. Ten-mile runs every week should have gone out with the Stone Age, or certainly the days when footballs weren't thought necessary for training. 'The boys will be keener to see the ball on Saturdays if they're starved of it in the week', was, I gather, the peculiar line of thinking behind that nonsense. No wonder our ball control took so long to match the continentals.

I'm not sure of the theory behind the long-distance running

unless there were ideas of pushing the lads for the Olympics in their spare time! No, we knew the way we played and trained was right for us – and, considering the trophies we've won with it, we can prove it. I was ready to make these feelings known to the directors, but I didn't have to. Good sense ruled their thinking and it wasn't necessary. Liverpool are sometimes worth following and there's no doubt a big part of their long run of success is because they have promoted from within, keeping the club stable. We had a good system, too, and had faith in it. So why change it?

When Colin Harvey was given the job, everyone was happy. That showed the extent of the respect he'd got throughout the club. We were made up for him and not just because he happens to be a nice fella. Of course, I might eat my words when he drops me! That's the fate of managers – players like you if they're in the side and hate you when they're not. Whatever, making him boss was right. We will win things under him. We realized how much he'd done for Everton. He was the main cog in the works that got things going in the slump. Whatever Howard's merits, and there were plenty, it could have been really bad for the club but for Colin taking a bigger hand in the crisis days. With all due respect to Mick Heaton, Colin made the backroom even stronger, promoting Terry Darracott and bringing back Mick Lyons. It has become a real family unit of Evertonians.

No players gave more in Everton's cause than them. Cut them and blue blood runs out. It was a great move for Lyonsy, coming back home after losing the tough manager's job at Grimsby. And Terry not only knows his stuff, but is also the life and soul of the party. I've said Colin was the best coach I've had and that but for him I might not have made it. But if I had the choice of taking anybody else to bring someone through the ranks it would be Terry. You can see just by the way he trains how much football has meant to him and how much he misses playing. The determination is so great it can almost be seen. No, Liverpool and the rest of football would be aware that although we'd lost a good manager the damage was small. It just meant that the family had closed ranks.

15

Wearing the Red

There's only one thing missing from my career, apart from having a go at the European Cup, and that's appearing in the last stages of the World Cup or the European Championship with Wales. And it hurts. Ex-manager Mike England has taken some flak about our failure to reach the big finals and has paid the price, but I don't believe we would have had to wait so long if the Welsh FA's thinking had not seemed to be dominated more by money than by glory. It's no coincidence that three times in four years between 1982 and 1986 we failed at the death at Cardiff and Swansea. Had any of those games with Iceland, Yugoslavia or Scotland been at Wrexham, I feel that players like Neville Southall and Ian Rush would have had their talents shown to the world in their proper setting; and I would have achieved a lifetime ambition. The players wanted Wrexham. The manager wanted Wrexham. The ones who stood out against us apart, of course, from the managements of Cardiff and Swansea, were a majority of the Welsh FA committee. And they were totally wrong.

I understand their motives. The FA are all but broke. They look at Cardiff's 42,000 capacity, compare it with the 28,500 at Wrexham and realize the difference could mean an extra

£40,000 revenue on the night. But it's the kind of thinking that reeks of lack of ambition, not to mention mistrust of the players. That amount of money would be more than made up for in the last stages of World Cup or European Championship. And what should be more important, making that £40,000 and not getting there, or putting Wales among the élite? I know what my answer is. The fact is that the Welsh FA have undermined their own players with that attitude. They are scared to death that we are not going to get through and that kind of feeling is transmitted. They have no faith in us to do the job, and that hurts.

Let's be honest. Wales' size and the small number of top class players available means that we're never going to be the greatest team the world's ever seen. We need every advantage we can get and to lose one of the biggest on the grounds of cash shows that priorities at the top are suspect. The Welsh FA have not played fair by the players or by the people who yearn to see us show what we can do in the major finals. This feeling for Wrexham isn't something that's just been plucked from the air. Nor is it a matter of North Wales bias. It is simply that it is no coincidence that we have not lost at the Racecourse ground in nearly a decade. Some of our best results in that time have been there. Think of Spain (3–0), England (1–0, 4–1), Rumania (5–0), BULGARIA (1–0), Finland (4–0). Nobody fancies facing us there. Why? There's nothing magic about the place. The secret lies in the people who go there and the atmosphere they produce. The simple fact is that they get behind us. And, strange as it may seem, that's not necessarily so at Cardiff or Swansea.

Local rivalries too often take priority over the national team in the south. The Cardiff fans are mainly there to see Cardiff players and it's the opposite at Swansea. In fact, Swansea fans won't go to Ninian Park and vice versa. It's 'we hate the Swans' or 'we hate the Cardiffs'. And that is not the right atmosphere for a national team effort. I want to see the Welsh FA have a drastic change of heart, make Wrexham the national stadium and put some money into it. I believe the South Wales lads would go along with that. Mike England had pushed hard over the years to make the FA aware of how important Wrexham is to us. Maybe it's getting to the stage when the players have got to do something about it.

Every Welshman feels bitter over the main reason for the Welsh FA's cash problems – the scrapping of the British championship. For 100 years it was part of our domestic soccer scene and I miss it and cannot understand why it's gone from the calendar. The Welsh and Irish always loved chopping down England and Scotland. Maybe it didn't happen that often, but when it did, it made it that much more special. Whatever happened, we made sure they earned their caps against us. It seems odd that nowadays England should have to scour the world looking for friendlies against such world powers as Colombia (!) when they've thrown away the chance of genuine domestic competition matches. Apparently, they don't class us as good enough to play them. Funny, that. It might have been true in the distant past but a look at the record books would tell them that standards have been evening up.

England have won sixty-two out of ninety-seven matches against us, but do you know how many of those came in the last eight meetings before they took us off the fixture list? Just three! And they only managed to beat us once in our last five visits to Wembley. On second thoughts, maybe it was because we were getting to close for comfort that they didn't want to know any more. So why has the British championship been killed off? Purely and simply because England weren't making money from 30,000 crowds at Wembley. But why did they restrict those matches to Wembley? There would probably be bigger crowds at Goodison, Anfield or Old Trafford to see Rushy and Mark Hughes take on Bryan Robson and co. It also seemed to me the health of the old four-way competition wasn't helped by packing it into a few days at the end of the season instead of spacing it through the campaign as had been done for years. That led to players, tired after some sixty games and nine months' effort, being expected to sparkle on hardening pitches. More than a few might have said, 'I think I'll miss this one, thank you.' No, the old competition deserved better than scrapping. What it needed was an understanding, intelligent format; but the men in power don't seem to have the brains or will to produce it.

Mike England suffered humiliations as Wales' boss that would have made others quit in disgust years ago. I'm not just talking about the fact he wasn't even consulted over our qualifying dates for the 1990 World Cup, a snubbing that has left us playing West Germany on the 31st May 1989, by which time the lads will have played fifty games after another tough season. He had his salary halved to £10,000 a year, a sum that's Fourth Division standard. His job was reduced to part-time status and seemed on the line every time we played. Last year he was slagged off by Welsh expatriates and called 'a clot' and 'thick' by Welsh FA secretary Alun Evans, who may have revealed his own true colours when making that ridiculous dinner-table attack. Thick? Mike's a smart enough business-man to be able to buy and sell Alun and his committee men a few times over, and wealthy enough to put his feet up for life if he wanted. That's my kind of thick! His 'crime' was to come within one good result of qualification for the finals of World Cup or European Championship four times in seven years. You'd think, given the criticism, he was boss of a team with England's resources instead of a small nation that for years relied for any success on the tremendous spirit players felt just by pulling on the red shirt of Wales.

I don't know which has been more amazing, the way he has been treated or the way he stayed in the job so long. I cannot think of another instance when a manager of a minor soccer power has been constantly carped at for not getting his team into major finals. Luxembourg's manager would probably get the freedom of the place if he won a match! OK, Billy Bingham has twice achieved miracles with Northern Ireland and Jack Charlton pushed the Republic of Ireland squad into this year's European Championship finals, but neither is expected to do that sort of thing. Their bosses only hope for it. Ours seemed to expect Mike to win the lot, which is ridiculous. You need luck as well as the rest of the necessities to even qualify and that is the one thing Mike has lacked. You only have to think back a few months to the game with Denmark in Copenhagen. How does a manager allow for a linesman's reflexes not being quick enough to allow him to spot an offside? That cost us our latest European qualification. And how does he legislate for Rushy, the world's deadliest finisher, missing chances he would normally swallow in the next game against the Czechs? Go back a bit further to another piece of heartbreak, the night our entry for the 1986 Mexico World Cup was stopped when a referee thought Dave Phillips' reflexes were doing more than allow his arms to protect his face against a shot hit from point blank range. Can a manager seriously be held responsible for that? Apparently, the Welsh FA believed so. Their reaction to that reprieve for Scotland was to hit him in the wage packet and, it is said, come within two votes of sacking him.

If I thought he had been wrong for the job I would have said so. And there's an obvious personal reason why I'd have started shouting if I'd thought it necessary. The same goes for Rushy and Nev Southall. Rushy, particularly. I know he's world class and, alongside Spain's vulture of a striker, Emilio Butragueno, the best centre-forward in the world, but I think he would become even greater if he had a world or European platform. But, even in all his disappointment at missing out, he has never suggested to me that he'd have stood a better chance if Mike had been pushed out.

There have been things on the fringe of this issue that have left me angry. I don't like it when people like John Toshack go yapping to the media and putting the boot in at the slightest excuse. I'm not sure how in touch he would be, based with Real Sociedad. And if he was touting for Mike's job, his method stank. Whatever his reason, there was nothing constructive in his blast. His only criticism seemed to be that the squad was a happy family. Maybe that's not part of his method. I seem to remember lads at Swansea didn't have a barrel of laughs when he was there. Really, what a load of tosh! The family thing has been one of Wales' strengths over the years. We fight as a family and that's why we're feared. That comes about because there are few players to pick from and we've turned the weakness into a strength. Toshack insults players like me when he talks of complacency. I'm ambitious and hungry. Those feelings don't go with complacency. If he feels frustrated about our near misses, how does he think we feel? In a way, he should understand more than most the position of a manager on small resources. Tosh's chances of breaking Spain's big-club monopoly are restricted, like Howard Kendall's at Bilbao, by his club's Basque-only rule.

As for the Welsh FA's position on Mike England, it left me baffled and disturbed. The manager should be left to run the team with full backing. Mike didn't have that. I don't think a clash of personalities with Alun Evans helped. We even had the feeling that certain people wanted us to lose just to hurt Mike. It was upsetting when stories about Mike's job being on the line nearly always appeared before matches. Why even hint his head is on the block at such a time? That's the last thing that should be on a player's mind before a big game. And where did these stories come from? Were they guesswork, or leaked from the committee? We should not be surprised at anything. Bear in mind, this is a body whose suggestions for improvement in the set-up are said to have included giving themselves track-suits for travelling, like the players, and querying whether the doctor was necessary. It doesn't take much thought to realize tracksuits would look ridiculous on them and since they are not exactly youngsters, I would have thought Dr Graham Jones was essential as a potential lifesaver! I know he has been just that for at least one of them. Mike was a wholehearted manager who did a good job. Maybe his trouble was that he spoke his mind. He is not a yes-man and I admire him for that, but plain speaking ruffles feathers. He must have been tempted to say 'stuff your job' many a time, but he is a great patriot and pride would have made him want to stay.

I'm not suggesting Mike England was the greatest manager to walk the planet. He's made his mistakes. And that's not surprising since he virtually had to learn as he went. His only previous management experience was in the very different, razzle-dazzle world of American soccer with Seattle Sounders. There were times, especially in his early days, when he allowed the pressure on him to affect his treatment of players seeming to pick on individuals to relieve his own frustrations. He once slagged off Jeff Hopkins after the lad had turned out for him as a favour. The Fulham defender had only dropped into the dressing-room to wish us luck before the World Cup qualifier with Iceland in Cardiff in November 1984, when he was dragged in as a sub because Alan Curtis had fallen ill. Jeff hadn't been in the squad and went on the bench stuffed with a Big Mac hamburger and a lager shandy, and wearing boots borrowed from Cardiff's boot room. Sure enough, Jeremy Charles was injured and Jeff was pitched on.

Not surprisingly, since he wasn't prepared, he didn't have the best of games, but when he came off at the end I couldn't believe the roasting Mike gave him. Jeff's face was a real sight. He'd done us a favour we'd won 2–1 and all he got was a slagging. Jeff was one of those lads Mike did seem to have a go at. I also went through a spell of that. But, if you're a favourite of his, that's it. Maybe not surprisingly, Rushy could do no wrong for him. Mike used to drool over him as if he were his dad and Rushy took some terrible stick over it. I remember one passing and control routine, involving a circle of players hitting the ball to a man in the middle who laid it off. Well, when I was in the middle, Rushy put the ball everywhere and I thought I did well to get a touch, let alone control it. But Mike said, 'Kevin, will you take care over your touch.' So, when it was Rushy's turn in the middle, I thought, 'Right, now I'll get him back.' So I started banging them everywhere. Next thing, Mike said, 'Kevin, make sure your passing's right for Rushy.' I held my head in my hands and Rushy laughed like a drain.

Nobody was laughing when Iceland gave Mike the worst moment of his management stint. His players were left shell-shocked. It will take years, or qualification for the 1990 World Cup, to get 14th October 1981, out of my mind. All we needed at Swansea that night was victory over the second weakest team in the five-team group and we were in the 1982 World Cup finals. Two countries went through. Russia were certainties and we'd put ourselves in a tremendous position to go with them. Our wins had included beating Czechoslovakia, and Turkey in Ankara before the most frightening crowd I've known. Another two points against a team we'd already beaten 4–0 would put us out of the Czechs' reach. There was so much confidence in the air that Mike even called us to a get-together at Lilleshall to discuss how we'd organise the finals pool. Young as I was, I thought that was a little stupid. It was too much like counting your chickens. Get there first, then start talking about such things. Our priorities were wrong. And everything else matched them on the night, starting with the selection.

It's easy to condemn Mike over that. I think he was wrong, but for good reasons. We were level with the Czechs, who had two tough games left against the Russians, but had a big advantage in goal difference. We knew there was small chance of improving the situation in our last game with Russia in Tbilisi so we needed a few against Iceland. But as Colin Harvey said when I got back to Everton, 'The worst thing you can do is go into a match talking about how many goals you're going to score.' And that's what we had done. We should have gone out, played our normal game and, if it was successful, the goals would have come. The priority is not to concede a goal. But there was none of that sort of talk in the papers. They were talking about how many we'd win by, which must have riled the Icelanders who were no mugs. Mike himself was bubbling in the dressing-room. 'We're going to get one,' he said, 'then we'll get another and another.' Nobody sounded a note of caution. Mike's line-up was based on Swansea's. They were flying at the time under John Toshack, using three at the back and five in midfield. He wanted Joey Jones and me to pick up the two strikers with Peter Nicholas sweeping.

Now I'm not a great believer in sweepers, especially the way we play, but if you are going to use one, he's got to be quick. And Nicholas, great midfielder though he is, is not fast and we were doubly hit because we missed having him in his best position. Robbie James did score after twenty-three minutes, but our formation left overcrowding in midfield and up front, and we didn't make quality chances. But we were geared up and still buzzing when the lights went out on us. Was that an omen? The Welsh FA seem to like having fixture clashes. They had managed to let this vital match coincide with Swansea playing rugby down the road. That meant 2,000 people were lost off the gate and, worse for us, the extra demand on electricity was apparently too much for the system. We were left kicking our heels in the dressing-room for forty-three minutes while power was restored. By the time it was, our adrenalin had evaporated and our concentration had gone.

Iceland hit us on the break a minute after half-time when Adgeir Sigurvinnson, then with Bayern Munich, equalized. Alan Curtis made it 2–1 but Sigurvinnson quickly levelled again with a tremendous shot after another break. We could do nothing about it and a night that had started in such high hopes and optimism ended in terrible anti-climax. As we were to produce no miracle in Russia, that was us out. Afterwards, there was dejection in the dressing-room and Mike had a go at some lads unnecessarily. They needed comforting not rollicking. There was no blame from us over the way he'd played it. It was only later, when you had time to think, that you realized it was wrong, and Mike knew it. We all learned from that. Even the Welsh FA accepted that it was part of the learning process in his first year and took it as one of those things. Despite that awful finish, we'd had a great year under him, including a 4–1 defeat of England. But what a difference victory would have made for Mike. Apart from having the freedom of Wales, it would have meant the backbiters that were to plague him would have laid low for longer. A few months later, we showed in Spain that we could have given the 1982 finals some quality. We went to Valencia and held the hosts, 1–1. It was one of our best performances. Robbie James scored and had a perfectly good 'goal' disallowed. We knew we were good that day because the fans pelted us with everything they could lay their hands on. But that wasn't much consolation for missing out on the big one.

We badly needed a smile after the Iceland nightmare but we didn't expect to get one in Russia. It wasn't funny knowing we had to get a result in Tbilisi to get us into Spain. Just going to the place in those days was no laughing matter. It meant a day's journey, ridiculous airport hold-ups and generally a load of hassle. As far as we were concerned, 'glasnost' and Mr Gorbachev were far away in 1981. The cold war was still pretty cold. But we found a secret weapon on that trip that we reckoned could have wrecked the Red Army without firing a shot. They'd have died laughing. We know because we tested it at Moscow airport and it was devastating. Mind you, it left us helpless as well!

Terry Boyle's passport photo looked pretty innocent. In fact, it was too innocent to be true. The Crystal Palace lad was twenty-three at the time but it made him look like a ten-year-old choirboy. And the fact that he wore one of those wide 'kipper' ties that were popular in the 1970s made it all the funnier. The lads were in hysterics just looking at it. It was absolutely nothing like him. We'd already spent about three hours getting through passport control before it was Terry's turn. Making the checks were two young, very serious-looking soldiers. They were typically thorough, but their efficiency started to crack when they got to Terry. They could not believe his picture was for real. Their expressions were a picture and that started us off again. They were shaking their heads, tapping on the glass of their booth and pointing at him as if to say 'is this really you?' By this time, the lads were falling about – and it was catching. The two young Russians actually started to laugh. They were human after all! But they didn't have long to show it. Within seconds, their door opened, they were yanked out and two other comrades pushed in to complete the job and let Terry through before they caught the 'disease'. Blow me, if the same thing didn't happen on the way back. You might have thought the guards would have been warned about the picture so there'd be no more risks to the military. But no, the two Russians duly broke up in their booth when they got hold of that passport and they, too, disappeared in the direction of Siberia!

Again, we needed that moment. We hadn't done the business in Tbilisi, losing 3–0, so there was to be no World Cup finals for us. On top of that, the journey home was a nightmare. The Russians might have been pretty good in space but their technology in those days did not extend to have good enough radar to get our plane through the Moscow fog. We were grounded for eight hours. And, back at the hotel, it took four hours just to get a phone call home to let Sharon know what had happened. When we did get back to the airport, we hadn't finished with the Russians. If they'd never seen a passport pic like Terry's, they'd certainly never dealt with anyone like Mickey Thomas.

We'd been waiting about an hour for our flight to be called when Mickey took a typical hand. He spotted an airport girl behind a glass screen heading towards the door we'd have to go through to get our plane. Straight away, Mickey was on his feet, saying 'right, here we go.' and headed for the door, followed by a queue of about 150 passengers. When he got to the door, he stopped dead, laughing his head off, and chortled, 'OK, I've got you all!' Of course, the girl he'd seen had nothing to do with our flight and everyone had to troop back to their seats, glowering and moaning. Nuts? of course, but it had been a bad journey and you need that sort of zaniness to keep you going sometimes.

Whenever Sheeds wants to wind me up, all he has to say is 'nine minutes . . . That's all you were away from the World Cup finals. Nine minutes . . .' That was the black September night in 1985 when we were deprived of the Mexico place we had earned by a refereeing decision I'll dispute until I have no more breath. Dave Phillips was doing no more than trying to protect himself when David Speedie let loose a shot that hit his hands but wasn't going to hit the goal. We had to beat Scotland and looked like doing it until Davie Cooper, who had revived the Scots, saved them with that eighty-first minute penalty. And that was the first time the desperation had gone from the Scots' eyes. We had been leading via Mark Hughes' early goal and they had not created one chance until Dutch referee Jan Keizer made his mark on the match. History had unforgivably repeated itself. Eight years before, the Scots had qualified against us for Argentina when they were given a penalty at Anfield for hands, and it was Joe Jordan who had handled!

We had set ourselves up for the chance of going to Mexico with two tremendous performances against Scotland and Spain after giving ourselves a mountain to climb. Our first two matches had been lost in Iceland (0–1) and Spain (0–3). We had struggled in Reykjavik where Neville Southall made a rare mistake for the goal in a force ten wind, and then we got trampled on in Seville. It was Emilio Butragueno's first game and he scored, but I'll remember it for the fact that I've never been in a match where so many things were happening off the ball – pushing, kicking, elbowing. I'm ashamed to say it provoked me into setting out to hurt someone for the only time in my career. Rincon, playing up front, was a bad little character who got on my nerves once too often when he punched me. He got stretchered off but even then got his revenge. From where I kicked him, he rolled twenty yards to the edge of our penalty box. The free kick was taken from there and they scored! It was also the game when Mark Hughes started alerting Barcelona to his potential. Rushy was out injured but Sparky took responsibility, giving the Butcher of Bilbao, Goicoechea, a hard time and had a nice 'goal' disallowed.

We broke our duck against Iceland – Jeff Hopkins' match – and then it was Scotland at Hampden. And here I've got to thank Tommy Docherty for helping spark one of Wales' all-time great showings. Doc really wound the lads up when he said we were only a four-man team. Four men? Ask Graeme Souness! Ask Kenny Dalglish! David Phillips made a pest of himself against Suey, stopping him doing anything, and Joey Jones, playing at centre-back that night, gave Kenny no respect at all. And I've never seen two centre-forwards work together as Rushy and Sparky did. They made Willie Miller and Alex McLeish wish they were back at Aberdeen. And Rushy's tremendous goal, the only one of the game, matched the performance. After that we wanted to get drunk for a month. Glasgow's never looked sweeter in the spring. We were so high that March night, it didn't even bother us much that our coach driver got us lost on the way to the airport. We missed our flight and had to go all the way home by coach. But I think we could have flown home without a plane.

The adrenalin was still flowing for the return with Spain in

Wrexham a month later. We also remembered what had been done to us over there. And it was nice to see some of them shaking their heads at us. Rincon was playing but got dragged off in the second half. Butragueno didn't play, Santillana was injured and Gordillo, a great player, was ordinary on the night. But we still had to go out and win it and we did, 3–0. Rushy scored twice but it was Hughes' fantastic flying volley that will stick in the memory and was probably the goal that won him his jackpot chance in Barcelona. Then, five months later, it was Scotland in Cardiff. Mike's last words were simple and direct. 'Go out there and do what you did at Hampden. Get stuck in and enjoy it!'

We were wound up because we had to win, but it was also an awkward situation for me. Sharpy was in their attack. He's a mate and it was difficult to go out with that hard feeling you must have for an opponent. I had to remind myself that I was playing for my country and that it was him or me for Mexico, and I was happy to see Pat Van den Hauwe take him. The Scots were so frightened of Rushy and Sparky after Hampden that they made Miller sweeper and played Richard Gough and McLeish as centre-backs. But when Sparky breached that defence early on it looked as if we were on our way at last. But maybe we scored too early. They had time to get it back, although they never looked like doing it until Cooper came on and started causing us bother down our right flank. Even then, they created nothing before that penalty sickener, and I thought Nev would have reached Davie's shot if the ground had not been greasy.

It wasn't only a bad night for us. Jock Stein, Scotland's legendary manager, suffered a heart attack and died fifty minutes after the match. I've never seen Graeme Souness so choked and that showed the sort of respect he had for the big man. It also says plenty for Jock that his death made us think about something other than our own misery. But you wouldn't be human if thoughts didn't return to your own troubles and I was especially sorry for Joey Jones whose last chance of a World Cup appearance had gone. But Joey's one of those happy-go-lucky chaps who won't be knocked down too long. Every day is a fresh start with him. Rushy took it badly and my mood matched his. It was only brightened when we went to a wine bar for something to eat and bumped into rugby stars Barry John and John Dawes. They bought us a drink and tried to make us feel better. I hadn't realized until then that the oval ball boys took that much interest in us. In fact, I hear Barry could have played soccer if he had wanted. He even took a football away with him when the rugby squad went on tours. The next day, despite the injustice of the result and decision, it was the same old story – Mike for the sack! If anyone should have got the blame it was us. Mike said we'd done everything right bar get the result. But we were there to do the business and we hadn't. If anyone should have been sacked after that it was the referee.

I know Wales are in danger of being labelled the 'nearly men' or even the 'maybe men' after missing out again in the 1987 European Championship. And I can understand the fans getting sick to death of hearing the same old excuses – dodgy goals, bad luck, missed chances. But that doesn't make them any the less true, as anyone who saw the last two games in Denmark and Czechoslovakia will vouch for. And when the backstabbers got to work on Mike England after we'd lost 1–0 in Copenhagen, the players went over the top. A tremendous 1-0 victory over the Danes in Cardiff a month earlier, in September, had left us needing two points from those last two games to qualify for the last stages in West Germany. We knew taking something from the Danes in the return would be hard – especially after their moaning and complaining over the first game. Not only are they one of Europe's most skilful teams, but they had threatened us with trouble after the way we'd set about them in Cardiff. The Danes are good players – if they have time to be! We went out to deny them that time, close them down fast and get our tackles in. They didn't like it one bit. In the end, they were only getting touched before they were falling over.

Ian St John accused us on his TV programme of kicking them, but what did he expect us to do – sit back and watch Morten Olsen, Preben Elkjaer and Michael Laudrup pass the ball about? There's no satisfaction in sharing a pitch with great players if you're losing 4-0. No, we were out there, proud to be Welsh and wanting to get to those finals. It should also be remembered that we had no Ian Rush. He was injured and feeling very low in Italy because he couldn't even travel, while his Juventus team-mate, Laudrup, who was also unfit, had been allowed by the club to play half the game. It didn't help Rushy that though they were good mates they hadn't spoken to each other for a week because of that big game coming up. All he could do was keep in touch by phone through the match and when we'd won, one of the press lads, Ken Gorman, held the phone out to the crowd so he could get a taste of the atmosphere. As it happened, we rode Rushy's loss. Mark Hughes played as if he had something to prove after being out in the cold for so long with Barcelona, He thrived on the extra responsibility and scored the vital goal. I rate Morten Olsen as special, but we made him look ordinary on the night. He wasn't happy and could hardly get off the pitch fast enough. Elkjaer went further. He threatened us in the tunnel about what we'd get in the return. I think he had wanted us to give him the ball and say, 'here you are. Have a shot. Hope you score.'

In Copenhagen, they certainly worked on getting Robbie James booked, which meant suspension for the next match. Mark Hughes was also cautioned, but it was no harder than you'd expect in such a big-stake game, and the crowd, painted faces and all, made the atmosphere one of the best I've played in. They were so good humoured that they were even singing cockney drinking songs. We decided not to hound the Danes this time. Our tactics were sound – to stay tight and solid against a crafty team who are always trying to pull you out of position. It worked so well that they hardly got a chance. And we had enough chances to have got a result, especially if Rushy's ankle had been at more than ninety per cent fitness. It was Elkjaer who had the last laugh that night, scoring a goal that should have been ruled out for offside long before he even got the ball. And that's how close we were to frustrating one of the continent's best. But, hard luck or no, it left us needing to win the final match in Czechoslovakia to qualify and you could almost see the knives sticking in the manager's back!

It didn't help when we'd heard that Welsh FA secretary Alun Evans had made some bad comments on radio. This he denied when Neville Southall confronted him to ask what the hell was going on; but we'd had enough. The players were so upset by the result and criticism that we called a quick team meeting at the airport. Then we pulled in Mike and told him, 'We're very upset by the comments that have been made. We want you to know we don't blame you for what has happened. As far as we're concerned, we can't get a better manager and if there is anything we can do to keep your job, we will.' He didn't take advantage of the offer as others might. All he said was, 'Don't worry about me. Worry about yourselves and don't do anything daft.' I suppose, with the mood we were in, we could have got into deep water if we'd really pushed it with the committee men who were there. Instead, we turned to the media for help, letting our feelings be known so that those in charge would have no doubt about how much we respected the man they had chosen. And we so nearly pulled off a miracle result for him in Prague.

It was just before that crucial game that John Toshack chose to make his hurtful newspaper attack on Mike. It angered not just me and the older players but also the younger squad members. There we were, going into the most important game of the series, and he helps prepare us by saying the manager should get the boot if we fail and that we're too comfortable. Mike was tight-lipped, but he was hurt. Who wouldn't be? What made it worse was that Tosh had been a team-mate of his more than a few times back in the seventies and I'd hate to think that in a few years' time someone who's playing alongside me now would stab me in the back like that. I don't know if there had been any bitterness between them, but there is now. And Mike is not the fella to get the wrong side of. We'd have loved to have rammed Tosh's words back down his throat in Prague. And we should have. The scoreline says 2-0 to the Czechs but as a guide to the game it's a liar. We had to go for broke and we did. Everything was right bar the result. Mike couldn't believe we could play so well and lose. We had ninety per cent of the game and ninety per cent of the chances and how we didn't win I'll never know. We could have been 4-0 up by half-time but nothing went right round the goalmouth.

It was a time when the greatest finisher in the world showed he was no machine. Put it this way, if Rushy had been playing against Everton, I'd expect him to have scored with every one. But it was a reflection on how much he wanted to make the finals that he was on the pitch at all. He was no more than sixty per cent fit with that ankle. Every morning when he woke it was sore but he had ice packed on it and just carried on. He wouldn't use it for an excuse, but he had every reason to cry off. So give him credit for being out there. A lot did cry off before that game. And I had an insight into Mike's difficulties when we sat down to discuss who else might come in when injuries struck. Apart from untried kids who could not be used in such a game, we came up with just four names. It's that shallow depth of talent that the critics should remember. A Welsh team manager can't just go out and buy players.

The difference in finishing was stark on the night. They had four chances and put away two. The first by Ivo Knoflicek, totally against the run of play, had a smell of offside about it – I know, again! And Michael Bilek killed us with a great curled free kick in the last minute. As for me, it wasn't only the result that was a sickener. I've never been so ill in a match. I threw up before and during the match after eating something which made me violently ill. The doc gave me a jab, but I kept being sick and at one point I thought I'd have to go off. But what really hurt was the fact we'd played so well and lost. If there was a consolation it was that Derby midfielder Geraint Williams came in and had a great debut.

But, really, there will be no rest or peace for any of us until we break this qualification bogey. It's no good harping on about what's gone except to try and learn from it as we go for the 1990 World Cup. The draw hasn't done us any favours – West Germany, Holland and Finland. But it will always be tough for us, as it has been for the Republic of Ireland, until we do break through and earn a higher seeding. But it will happen, and if I have my way it will be this time. I'll be at my peak and so should Rushy and Sparky Hughes. You can bet that none of those countries will relish facing us. But what I really want to hear at the end of this series is Ruud Gullit, Rudi Voller and co going away squealing about our luck, our offside goals and their missed chances.

16

Taking Time Out

It's as well I got the 1987–88 season out of the way before my testimonial. I wouldn't like to have had that anti-climax as part of my big year. Back in August, I couldn't see any reason why we shouldn't keep the title we'd had to fight so hard to win in 1987. And we desperately wanted to give Colin Harvey something memorable to mark his first season as boss. Instead, we finished up giving him little but heartache, watching the other lot across the park walk away with our crown. Not only that. They stopped us winning the FA Cup when we thought our names were on it. And we got knocked out of the semi-final of the Littlewoods Cup when we fancied that as a little consolation for what was happening to us in the League. On a personal note, I was saddened when Mike England, the man who'd given me my big chance on the international scene, was sacked by Wales. And I finished up a frustrated spectator for the last few months after collecting a deep-seated groin injury, the worst I've ever had.

Where did it all go wrong? Don't lay the blame at Colin's door. He had a lot to lose when he took over from Howard Kendall. He'd won a tremendous reputation as a coach and motivator, and deserved it. Now he was being asked to make that extra step which has been one too much for some people. Well, I've seen nothing to suggest it will be too much for him. Maybe he's got a bigger car and wears a suit and tie a bit more, but those are about the only changes I've seen in him. The style is the same and so is the way he lives. His relationship with the players is no different, apart from calling him 'boss'. The routine hasn't changed. Everything is as it was when he and Howard were together. And that's good. If you've stayed with me this far you'll know my respect for the way we've trained and gone about things. It's been the key to our success and will be again. No, if any man will get it right for us, it's Colin. And Liverpool know it! His great tests will be the quality of his buying and the need to keep happy a big squad of ambitious, talented players. Neither is easy. Evertonians will expect him to at least match what Liverpool have done in the market. Anything less wouldn't improve what we've got. I'm talking about a Rush or a Lineker. And how many of those are around? Nobody likes playing in the reserves, especially established players, and the only way to keep that kind of competition in the club is through the pocket. Perhaps that's how Liverpool have managed to keep their players happy over the years.

Some will say we lost out when Liverpool's reply to our 1987 triumph was to spend most of the £3.2 million Juventus paid for Ian Rush on Peter Beardsley and John Barnes – and then find another £900,000 for Ray Houghton. That was ambitious. Why didn't we spend? The short answer is we didn't have to. The championship squad was still together. Paul Bracewell, we thought, was gradually getting his fitness back. And we surely couldn't have similar injury problems to those we'd beaten the previous year. Couldn't we? We actually had more players playing this time when they weren't fit! And we couldn't quite find the answer to that, especially not without Kevin Sheedy, who was dogged by one injury after another and missed most of the campaign. If we'd had a full squad there wouldn't have been such a gap between Liverpool and us. Maybe no gap at all! Apart from the injuries, it doesn't take A-levels to know where we've suffered. Defensively, we were almost as good as Liverpool. But we just didn't score the goals they did. That's where we went wrong. And you can't just put the blame on the strikers or on one player. Graeme Sharp scored over twenty goals again; Adrian Heath and Wayne Clarke both got into double figures. But overall, we didn't create enough chances, which is a collective thing. And when we did, not enough were put away. Also, some players didn't hit the form they'd like. For instance, Ian Snodin found it hard coming up from the Second Division. People will say that an £840,000 player ought to be able to slot straight in, but that's easy to say. Snowy will know he must get involved more, but I've seen enough to know he's got the qualities of a great player.

There's also the fact Liverpool had a one-off season in a First Division which, as Bob Paisley said, was not as good as in previous years. All credit to them. They've done really well. But I can't see them going through so many games undefeated as they did last time. Despite all the rave reports, they're not the best Red side I've faced. But they have class men like John Barnes who can turn games with one bit of magic. Twice he did us last season when we thought we had them beaten. I didn't think he'd be a Liverpool player, but if anybody was going to get real consistency out of him it was them. Now he's got everything, not least marvellous balance which means he never seems to fall in a tackle. Stevie McMahon also had a great season. I wanted him to do well after being brought up with him as a player. I always look to see if he's scored and if he has and it's on TV, make a point of watching. The only thing about him that has surprised me is that it was so long before England realized what he could give them. I don't know if it was his temper, or the way he played the game, but it took him two years at Liverpool to be recognized by his country, which is a shame. He may be losing his hair, but he's gained everywhere else and I'm glad he's done it. Not for Liverpool but for Stevie because I admire him. He's a winner and that's the type every side needs. Maybe he's one of the reasons why too many teams are frightened of having a go at Liverpool. We showed what could be done against them. If they're scared of anybody it's us. But they have set the standard for everybody, just as we did the previous year.

Deep down, we knew the League was over months before Liverpool actually clinched it, although there was no way we would even think of admitting it. Now it's up to the rest of us to get up there and do something about it. And we will. I can see us challenging again hard next season and there are a few others in with a shout. Manchester United didn't get much credit for finishing second. True, they didn't impress anyone until the final stages, but the foundations may be there for a real challenge this time. Spurs won't go on sleeping with Terry Venables there. They have the money and he has the continental connections to make spectacular signings. Arsenal keep getting closer, and Cloughie's got those young lads doing well for him at Forest. But he's had a few teams like them, looking as if they're going to do something, then fading away. These may be different. There are good players there and they came close in the FA Cup semi-final with Liverpool. The questions they need to answer are whether they've been put in too quick and whether the kids can do it the second time around, when something will be expected of them.

As for me, I've approached the new campaign by spending the summer making sure the injury will be right for the big kick-off. And here I want to pay tribute to the patience and understanding of my wife Sharon who's had to suffer through all my moods over not being able to get on the pitch. There must have been times when she was fed up to the teeth, but she realizes what football means to me. Maybe only another footballer's wife will know what she suffers.

I wish I could be as certain Wales will solve their problems as I am about Colin solving Everton's. The goings on since Mike England got the bullet don't fill me with a lot of optimism. I thought the Welsh FA were utterly wrong to get rid of him in the first place, but once they'd decided he was going to carry the can for not achieving miracles surely the thing was to have the appointment of a successor ready to announce to the world. I expected somebody to be named. I thought they had somebody. Instead, with another World Cup qualification tournament starting, it has seemed a question of who hasn't been talked about in connection with the job! Cloughie had his supporters, but most Welshmen wanted a fellow-countryman to be appointed. There's something about playing in that red shirt which only a Welshman can understand. Terry Yorath could do the job, but whether he could cope with managing Swansea and Wales I don't know. It was important a successor should have been named quickly. Every manager has his own way of playing, so whoever it was to be needed to have the team that opens the World Cup qualifying group against Holland this autumn to be playing the way he wants. One thing is certain. Whoever is chosen has the same problems as Mike – you've only got so many players to choose from. Terry found that out the hard way when he took charge against Sweden at the back end of last season. With Pat Van Den Hauwe and me out, he had to put midfielders Mark Aizlewood and Kenny Jackett at centre-back. Both are good players, but not central defenders and not the quickest.

If Wales' future is uncertain, I've got to the point where I must think long and hard about mine. This season most of my spare time will be wrapped up in my testimonial, but at the end of it, my contract is up. I'll be twenty-eight and the next deal I sign will be very important because it will probably be my last big one. And it'll be a time to do what's best for Sharon and the kids. I'd love to see my days out at Everton. But that will be up to the club. I've been a life-long Evertonian and I still feel the same about the place as when Dad used to stand me on my soap-box to watch Alan Ball at Goodison. I don't think he'd support me playing for anyone else! But when you've got the family's financial security to consider the deal has to be right. It's only this year I've started seriously thinking about what I'm going to do after I finish playing. And at the time of writing I still have no clear idea although the way I feel right now I'd like to stay in the game, but not as a manager. Maybe I might change my mind in five years' time, but at the moment I don't want that hassle. Coaching's more my scene.

It's a time when thoughts of Italy and Spain cross your mind. Everybody dreams of the security a move there means, as it has for Rushy and Gary Lineker. And it would be nice to go out there and experience a different way of life. The playing challenge would appeal to me, too. Rushy tells me Italians think the Brits are rubbish at defending. I'd like to think I could prove them wrong. In fact, I think it's easier to defend in their game. They can happily dive into tackles knowing there's always a sweeper behind to pull them out of the mire. Over here, we can't do that because you know you're the last man in defence. Not many British defenders get the chance to prove what I'm saying, but I've no burning desire to do it and I must say it won't bother me if I don't. Anyway, I think people have got me and Everton so bound up together they don't expect me to play for anybody else. Maybe that's why you never hear gossip connecting me with another club. For the moment, all I'm thinking about is getting back our number one spot. It's an unbelievable feeling holding that old championship trophy and I just fancy making it a hat-trick in my testimonial year. . . .